Pivotal Pennsylvania

Presidential Politics from FDR to the Twenty-First Century

G. Terry Madonna
Franklin & Marshall College
Center for Politics and Public Affairs

Pennsylvania History Studies Series, No. 31
Pennsylvania Historical Association
Mansfield, Pennsylvania
2008

COVER: President Franklin Roosevelt rides with Pennsylvania politicians Senator Joe Guffey and Governor George Earle to a campaign rally at the state capitol in Harrisburg days before the 1936 election. (Pennsylvania State Archives: MG-342, George Howard Earle Papers)

Printed by
Huggins Printing Company
2900 Sycamore Street
Harrisburg, PA 17111

Table of Contents

Editor's Introduction

Each presidential election year, it has become common to hear Pennsylvania described as a "battleground state." In a nation with many states firmly held by either the Democrats or the Republicans, Pennsylvania elections have been closely contested. As a result, candidates visit Pennsylvania communities frequently, political commercials demand our attention, and our telephones ring with appeals from candidates. Yet this was not always the case. A century ago, Pennsylvania was so firmly controlled by one political party – the Republicans – that such competitiveness would have seemed unimaginable. How and why did the electoral balance shift? When did Pennsylvania become so pivotal in the nation's politics?

For answers to these questions, the Pennsylvania Historical Association turned to one of the state's leading political analysts, G. Terry Madonna. Many readers will be familiar with Professor Madonna from his newspaper columns, interviews on radio, and appearances on television. As director of the Franklin & Marshall College Poll, Professor Madonna tracks and keeps Pennsylvania voters informed about current trends in politics. For this volume, we have asked him to look back and explain how we came to hold such a prominent place in presidential elections. During this election year, 2008, the Pennsylvania Historical Association is pleased to provide such an authoritative, richly detailed account of presidential politics in Pennsylvania from FDR to the twenty-first century.

Charlene Mires
Villanova University

Preface and Acknowledgements

The purpose of this volume is to provide a concise and clear history of Pennsylvania presidential elections since 1932. During this period, the state became very competitive not only in presidential elections but in other statewide elections as well. After 130 years of one-party rule, it became a valued prize in the Electoral College sweepstakes. In the course of writing about nineteen elections, I have tried to integrate presidential campaigns in the state within the context of the larger national picture.

First I would like to thank the editor, Professor Charlene Mires, for tolerating several missed deadlines and her encouragement throughout the preparation of this manuscript. My two undergraduate research assistants at Franklin & Marshall College, Bradly Nankerville and Lindsey Harteis, performed yeoman-like work locating sources and checking data tirelessly. At Villanova University, graduate student Hillary S. Kativa assisted with editing and illustration research. The final product benefited from scrutiny and suggestions from my friend and long-time colleague Professor John McLarnon of Millersville University. Lastly, but most importantly, my thanks to my wife Maribeth Madonna who patiently allowed me to miss too many family functions while completing the research and writing of the manuscript. Naturally any defects in the content and infelicity in style belong exclusively to me.

G. Terry Madonna
Lancaster, Pennsylvania

Introduction

From the very beginning of the two-party system in the 1790s, politics in Pennsylvania has shown a complexity and diversity not seen in many other states. In part, the complexity stems from the historic settlement patterns that began in the seventeenth century and continued into the late nineteenth century. The diversity stems from the multiplicity of ethnic and religious groups that settled in the state. Until the 1960s, however, one-party domination characterized politics in Pennsylvania for extended periods of time.

For the first sixty years of the nineteenth century, the Democrats held the state in an iron grip. During the first party system, starting roughly from Thomas Jefferson's election in 1800 and continuing to James Monroe's in 1820, the Democratic Republicans, as the Democrats were then known, succeeded in delivering the state's Electoral College vote for their candidates in every election. The state was so solidly Democratic that it earned the reputation, "the key stone in the democratic arch." Their opponents, the Federalists, provided virtually no statewide opposition after the War of 1812. By the 1820s, politics became a battle among factions of Democratic Republicans. The contentious and divisive 1824 election resulted in the House of Representatives electing a president, John Quincy Adams, for the second time in twenty-four years. It also caused the disintegration of the Democratic Republican Party. Deeply divided, the party split into two factions that soon reconstituted themselves in the second party system of Democrats and Whigs.

Beginning in 1824, Andrew Jackson easily carried the popular vote in Pennsylvania in three straight elections, propelling the emergence of the Democratic Party. Between 1825 and 1828, Jackson's supporters in the state were prime movers in creating the modern Democratic Party. In the inter-party competition that emerged after 1832 with the formation of the Whig Party, the Democrats continued to dominate presidential elections, losing the state only twice to Whig candidates. Both of the Whigs were "war hero" candidates. William Henry Harrison, "Old Tippecanoe," won in 1840 by a mere 2,881 votes, and Zachary "Old Rough and Ready" Taylor won in 1848 by 13,538 votes. The Democrats went on to carry the state for native-son James Buchanan in 1856, and then the balance shifted. Nineteen elections would come and go before the Democrats could again win the state for their presidential nominee.

Following the Civil War, the Republican Party gained vise-like control of Pennsylvania politics and did not relinquish it until the New Deal years in the 1930s. From 1876 to 1892, the party put together the organizational and financial elements for virtually complete control, but presidential elections remained close

A souvenir plate from the 1906 Republican National Convention commemorates past party luminaries and current leaders. Throughout the nineteenth century, the Republicans dominated Pennsylvania presidential politics and state politicians frequently played the role of kingmaker for the party's nominees. (Temple University Libraries, Urban Archives)

and hard-fought. During this period, the Republican presidential winners averaged 52 percent of the popular vote in Pennsylvania, and none exceeded 53 percent.

The Republican trend in the state gained considerable reinforcement during a major realignment of voters in the 1890s, when the party increased its voter-base in the state's urban areas. Between the 1890s and the 1930s, the Republicans extended their control over every aspect of the politics and government of the state. Eleven consecutive Republican governors were elected between 1899 and 1934. One Democratic nominee in 1930 withdrew from the ticket to seek the office of Grand Exalted Ruler of the Elks rather than face what appeared to be certain electoral defeat. Every U.S. senator representing the state until 1934 was Republican. From 1885 until 1934, the Republicans controlled the State House of Representatives, and the same was true for the State Senate from 1880 until 1936 – the longest period of time any party had led either chamber in state history.

At the county level, two-thirds of Pennsylvania counties regularly voted Republican. And contrary to the voting habits of many other northeastern cities, the state's two largest cities were Republican strongholds – Pittsburgh (until 1932) and Philadelphia (until 1951). It could be truly said that Pennsylvania was the most Republican of the large industrial states.

From the end of the Civil War until the early 1920s a trio of political leaders successively led the Republican Party: Simon Cameron, Matthew Quay, and Boies Penrose. The three epitomized the political bosses of the times. They decided who would run for office and who would get state and federal jobs. They were powerful enough to dictate the policies of the state legislature. They also were kingmakers in the presidential sweepstakes, participating in the secret meetings and the backroom deal-making that dominated the presidential nomination process well into the twentieth century.*

The Republican Pennsylvania kingmakers were effective because of the one-party nature of the state's politics. The large size of Pennsylvania's electoral vote gave the state added importance in the nomination of presidential candidates. The kingmakers used the favorite son technique as a tactical maneuver to strengthen the state's negotiating position at national conventions. They put forward favorite sons as presidential candidates in order to hold the large state delegation together for the purpose of negotiating patronage advantages – jobs and appointments in any new administration. This tactic also held open the prospect that a deadlocked convention might actually nominate a Pennsylvania favorite son.

*See the earlier volume in the Pennsylvania History Studies Series, Robert G. Crist, ed., *Pennsylvania Kingmakers* (State College, Pa.: Pennsylvania Historical Association, 1985).

Chapter 1
The Democrats Emerge: the 1930s

The Great Depression brought about a great national experiment following the 1932 election. Known as the New Deal, the national programs passed by Congress at the behest of President Franklin D. Roosevelt produced the most profound change in the nation's politics since the 1896 election. Politically, the popularity of Roosevelt and the New Deal caused a realignment of millions of voters into the Democratic Party. The groups shifting to the Democrats included immigrants, many from southern and eastern Europe, who migrated to the United States in large numbers during the first years of the twentieth century. A second group of new Democrats were African Americans, especially those in the urban areas of the North, who had been Republicans since the Reconstruction period but now followed Pittsburgh publisher Robert L. Vann's admonition in 1932 to "go turn Lincoln's picture to the wall." Soon Democratic leaders were arguing that black voters had remained in the debt of Republicans for too long. David L. Lawrence, a political leader and future governor, complained in a speech to a black audience in 1933 that Republicans had received votes faithfully from blacks for the Emancipation Proclamation, but they had given blacks precious little in return. In addition to immigrants and African Americans, the Democrats held onto their old voting blocs, particularly white Protestants in the South. Many new voters, often the sons and daughters of immigrants who had just come to maturity, contributed to the new majority as well. Roosevelt ultimately was elected president four times and his Vice President Harry Truman one time largely as a result of this profound alteration of the nation's political system.[1]

Within Pennsylvania, the Great Depression and the New Deal profoundly affected the state's politics. The Republicans' post-Civil War dominance reached a high point in 1928, when 65 percent of the state's vote went for their presidential candidate, Herbert Hoover. Hoover again carried the Keystone State in 1932, but the New Deal and the personal popularity of FDR caused the Republicans' share of the presidential vote to drop to 41 percent in 1936, a truly stunning reversal within an eight-year period. At the same time, the Democrats increased their share from 34 percent to 57 percent, an equally stunning 23-point increase.

Another significant change resulted from an urban-rural alignment of Pennsylvania voters. Through most of the 1920s, until the 1928 campaign of Democratic presidential candidate Alfred E. Smith, the Democratic vote tended to come from the rural parts of the state. But the Smith candidacy and the New Deal produced a new alignment, with Democrats drawing an increasing share of votes

Interior view of 1928 Democratic candidate Alfred E. Smith's campaign headquarters in Philadelphia. While Smith lost the election, his status as a New York City native drew increased Democratic votes from urban areas and help lay important groundwork for the subsequent New Deal coalition. (*Philadelphia Record* photograph, Historical Society of Pennsylvania)

from urban areas. Smith's appeal to urban voters came from his Irish ethnic roots, his Catholicism, and his opposition to Prohibition. Although he lost the election, Smith substantially increased Democratic votes in urban areas, especially those with high concentrations of new immigrants. Nationally, he won the twelve largest cities by more than 300,000 votes, the same cities Republican Calvin Coolidge had won by 1.3 million votes in 1924. Smith's gains also took place in Pittsburgh and Philadelphia, presaging the New Deal realignment that created the new Democratic majority after 1932.

A close examination of the presidential votes in Philadelphia during the decade of the twenties offers some compelling evidence of the rise of the Democratic Party even before the New Deal. The Democratic candidate in 1920, James Cox, was swamped in the city by more than 217,000 votes. In 1924 John W. Davis lost to Calvin Coolidge by almost 300,000. In 1928, with an enlarged electorate as more immigrants achieved citizenship, Smith increased the

Democratic vote from 54,000 in 1924 to 277,000 in 1928 – a five-fold increase – and pushed the Democrats to 40 percent of the vote in the city. Franklin Roosevelt did even better in the Great Depression election of 1932. He lost the city by only 70,000 votes. Democrats made their greatest gains in those parts of Philadelphia with the highest concentrations of foreign-born voters. In Pittsburgh, a similar story can be told. Smith lost the city by only a few thousand votes. FDR carried the city in 1932 by 24,000 votes, in an election in which the Steel City broke from Republican control and became a New Deal Democratic city, beginning the transition to a politically competitive state. In the 1936 presidential election, urban Philadelphia and Allegheny counties contributed 35 percent of the state's total vote, and the Democrats won 60 and 65 percent, respectively.[2]

1932: Roosevelt and Hoover

The central issue in the 1932 presidential campaign was, of course, the Great Depression. In 1929 the stock market crash precipitated – but fundamentally did not cause – the worst economic downturn in American history. Economic indicators tell an important, but not complete, story of the impact the Depression had on Americans. At its nadir in 1932-33, industrial production fell more than 50 percent. Almost 13 million workers were unemployed; another 13 million were underemployed, and more than a million people roamed the nation in search of any kind of work. Some sold apples on the streets of the big cities before returning to their makeshift hovels set up in some cases in dumps and empty lots – which were often scornfully referred to as "Hoovervilles."

In Pennsylvania an estimated 16 percent of the adult population was out of work. Bank failures were rampant. Beginning almost daily in the early 1930s, almost five hundred closed their doors before the Depression's ravages ended. Times were so tough that the state legislature actually reduced its own salary for the first and only time in history, but a personal battle between independent Republican Governor Gifford Pinchot and Republican political leaders prevented the state from developing an effective Depression response. Before 1932 came to an end, the infighting spilled over to the presidential election.

Under these circumstances the Republicans, facing certain defeat, renominated Hoover. To do otherwise would have meant recognizing the complete failure of the administration to combat the Depression. Interestingly, Hoover's Depression-fighting measures, though not successful in mitigating the Depression, were more vigorous and expansive than any other president in American history. Nevertheless they were grossly inadequate in scope and federal commitment.

By 1932, the Democrat gaining the most national attention for his Depression-fighting measures was Franklin D. Roosevelt. As Governor of New York, his state led the nation in programs to combat the worst features of the Great Depression by expanding state services and presaging many of the ideas that would comprise the New Deal. His reelection as governor in 1930, with a majority unparalleled in New York history, virtually assured him of the Democratic nomination in 1932.   FDR also had become a major player in the Democratic Party; he had nominated Al Smith in 1924 and 1928 and brokered some of the party's internal controversies. Born into a patrician family, a distant cousin of Theodore Roosevelt and a Harvard graduate, he had served as assistant secretary of the Navy under Woodrow Wilson. In 1920 he was his party's vice presidential candidate in a losing campaign in which he and presidential candidate James Cox lost to Warren G. Harding and Calvin Coolidge. Not even a case of polio in 1921 halted his political ambition or his electoral success.

Roosevelt was the first Democrat to seek his party's nomination in 1932, but being first and being a successful governor of the largest state in the union did not guarantee an easy nomination. He had to contend with several rivals, including John Nance Garner, the 61-year-old Speaker of the House, who had the support of newspaper tycoon William Randolph Hearst. Another major rival was the 1928 Democratic nominee, Al Smith.

The various candidates battled through a series of state primaries. FDR, however, was the only candidate with the resources to wage a national campaign, and he was careful not to offend any of the state favorite son candidates, especially avoiding confrontation in Pennsylvania. Roosevelt had considerable support in the Keystone State. The most active and important Pennsylvania backer was Joseph F. Guffey. The Greensburg Democrat had begun communicating with Roosevelt as early as 1930, and he traveled to Albany in 1931 to meet with the governor and pledge the allegiance of the state Democratic delegation. Guffey was the first leader of a big state other than New York to endorse Roosevelt. A multimillionaire oil man, Guffey had worked in the administration of Woodrow Wilson, who had been his professor during his student days at Princeton University. They developed a long and lasting friendship. More important to FDR was Guffey's leadership of the Pennsylvania Democratic Party and his activity as a member of the Democratic National Committee. Later, he also played a major role in reinvigorating the Pennsylvania Democratic Party during the New Deal years, and in 1934 he became the first Democratic senator elected from Pennsylvania in sixty years.

Roosevelt, nonetheless, did not win the Pennsylvania's national convention delegation without a fight. A viable stop-Roosevelt movement, organized in the state as early as 1931, had formidable leaders: John Collins, then the state Democratic chairman, and Sedgwick Kistler, a national party committeeman. Ostensibly backing another run by Al Smith, their real purpose was to find a Pennsylvania favorite son to support. Notwithstanding the effort, Roosevelt won the ensuing Pennsylvania primary, electing 50 of the 72 contested delegates to the national convention.

The intrigue at the convention, held in June in Chicago, centered on control of the convention machinery and the nomination struggle. Despite the Pennsylvania primary results, the state's delegates were very much in the thick of the debate. The 76 votes were not officially pledged, and competition for them was fierce. On the first ballot, FDR fell 104 votes short of the nomination, and he received 44.5 of Pennsylvania's votes. On the fourth and final ballot, the Pennsylvania vote for Roosevelt rose to 55, the most cast for him by any state.[3]

During the fall campaign, Roosevelt talked about recovery but provided no specifics as to how he would conquer the Great Depression. His campaign did, however, promise a New Deal – which he called a "fundamental reappraisal of values" – and he called for bold, persistent experimentation to end the economic slide. Perhaps as important as any ingredient in FDR's campaign was his style, which contrasted sharply with Hoover. FDR radiated confidence, humor, and optimism that the economy could be righted, while Hoover's gloomy and colorless manner had all the markings of a beaten man.

For the first time since 1856, Democrats were optimistic that their presidential candidate might carry the state. Pittsburgh's Democratic City Chairman, David Lawrence, organized one of FDR's more memorable visits to Pennsylvania during the fall campaign. FDR arrived in Pittsburgh on October 19 for a rally at Forbes Field, where he addressed 50,000 enthusiastic fans. On his way to Forbes from the train station, thousands of people lined the streets – schools had been canceled, and local bands played along FDR's route. The future president gave his traditional speech, decrying the nation's joblessness and the growing federal deficit. He received his largest ovation when he promised to end Prohibition, a popular theme in western Pennsylvania. He also criticized the growing federal deficit under Hoover. That would later haunt FDR when New Deal spending made short shrift of government frugality and deficits. But that mattered little to the passionate Roosevelt fans in Pittsburgh. A gleeful Lawrence predicted a 100,000-vote margin in the Steel City.[4]

The Republicans realized the state was up for grabs. Normally Pennsylvania was taken for granted, given the past loyalty of the state's voters to the party's presidential candidates. Now, taking no chances, Republican leaders sent vice-presidential nominee Charles Curtis into the state for a whirlwind campaign. Among other disadvantages they faced in 1932, the Republicans needed outside help because Republican Governor Gifford Pinchot was not in Hoover's camp. Pinchot had been reelected to a second term as governor of Pennsylvania in 1930. There had been a brief flirtation with a Pinchot presidential effort in 1931; he received letters and personal solicitation from all over the country. He had no national party support, however, and he declined a quixotic presidential campaign.

In 1932 Pinchot refused to campaign for Hoover and stayed silent throughout the campaign. The governor personally knew and admired Roosevelt, but more important was his view that the Hoover administration had been ineffective in dealing with the country's massive unemployment. Pinchot was also at odds with other Republican leaders in Pennsylvania, including a longstanding feud with the party's Philadelphia boss, William S. Vare. During Pinchot's first term he had refused to certify Vare's election to the U.S. Senate in 1926, and the bitterness with Vare and other leaders grew worse over time. So it was not surprising when the Republican-controlled legislature opposed his proposals to combat the Depression, notably on utility and tax legislation. These lawmakers essentially took orders from their county political leaders, which meant Pinchot was in a feud with the politicians who pulled the strings of their state lawmakers as well. No leader was more important than Delaware County political honcho and state senator John McClure, and the governor's differences with the senator broke into the open just days before the election. McClure tried to lure the governor into stating his choice for president by sending him a letter pointedly asking for his position. Pinchot did not respond, but when the governor was a no-show for the Republicans' final campaign event at the state capital, there was little public doubt that he was not supporting Hoover.[5]

As the campaign came to a close, the Republicans launched a furious get-out-the-vote endeavor. They held rallies in all sixty-seven county seats on the Saturday before the election, with one thousand mini-rallies spread out over the following two days. The party orchestrated five hundred speakers at these events. The high point was a campaign stop by President Hoover at Philadelphia's Reyburn Plaza, which drew a crowd that the *Philadelphia Inquirer* estimated at 100,000 supporters.[6]

However, the national election outcome was never in doubt. Roosevelt buried Hoover, winning the popular vote 57 percent to 40 percent, while his party captured both chambers of Congress. In the new Congress the majorities were significant: the Senate, 60 to 35, and the House, 310 to 117. The turnout in 1932 was substantially lower than turnout in 1928. FDR carried forty-two states and Hoover six, and all of Hoover's states were in the Northeast. Hoover won only 59 electoral votes to Roosevelt's 472.

Pennsylvania contributed 36 of Hoover's 59 electoral votes, and it was the largest state carried by Hoover. Hoover barely won a majority of the popular vote, 51 percent to FDR's 45 percent. Roosevelt managed to win twenty-seven counties, reversing the disastrous slide the Democrats had seen during the 1920s, when in all three presidential elections the Democratic nominees carried only a combined ten counties. Important counties won by FDR in 1932 included Allegheny, Beaver, Lackawanna, Fayette, Cambria, and Luzerne – all with large recent immigrant populations. In Allegheny County, FDR won by 37,000 votes, far below the

100,000 projection of Chairman Lawrence, but a victory for a Democratic presidential candidate for the first time since the Civil War. As expected, FDR swept the working-class, Catholic wards in Pittsburgh, and he did better than in the past among black voters. The day after the election an ecstatic Lawrence predicted the demise of the Republican Party in the city. The 1932 election marked the transition of Pittsburgh from Republican to Democratic control. In Philadelphia, FDR was less successful, but still he reduced the Democratic loss to 71,000 votes.

The 1932 election and the advent of the New Deal began the transformation of the state into genuine two-party competition. Building on the growth of their voter support in 1932, the Democrats won two major statewide offices two years later, electing Roosevelt's friend Joseph Guffey to a U.S. Senate seat and George H. Earle to the governorship.

1936: Roosevelt and Landon

Roosevelt's first term was dominated by efforts to combat the Great Depression. The president, using ideas generated from his advisers, initiated the first New Deal, a welter of thirteen economic recovery programs begun within the first one hundred days of his term. These programs mitigated but did not end the economic turmoil in the country, and FDR was soon attacked politically from both the right and the left. From the right he was accused of wrecking capitalism by supporting pro-labor policies and handouts to the poor. From the left he faced criticism that his programs had not gone far enough. These liberal critiques spawned movements headed by three critics: Senator Huey Long, who proposed a confiscatory tax scheme to provide a guaranteed income to American families; Francis Townsend, a retired dentist, who proposed a pension for older Americans; and Father Charles Coughlin, a Catholic priest with a weekly radio program, whose 30 million listeners heard advice that FDR should expand the New Deal by nationalizing banks and destroying the "money powers." The three developed sizable followings that threatened to destabilize the New Deal and posed a threat to FDR's reelection in 1936. At the same time, a series of court decisions shut down some of FDR's most important recovery programs. As a result, he initiated in 1935 the second New Deal aimed more at fundamental reform than recovery, and he included among its five major programs the law creating Social Security. The Democrats were now riding a crest of popularity and eagerly looking forward to the 1936 election.

Faced with overwhelming odds, the Republicans nominated the progressive-minded governor of Kansas, Alfred M. "Alf" Landon. Landon was a Pennsylvanian by birth, having been born in 1887 in West Middlesex in Mercer County, but his family moved to Kansas by way of Ohio when he was 17. Surprisingly, he returned to little West Middlesex – to his boyhood home – to launch his presidential campaign.

Preparing to re-nominate President Franklin Roosevelt at the 1936 Democratic National Convention in Philadelphia, members of the Pennsylvania delegation jubilantly gather outside Convention Hall. (*Philadelphia Record* photograph, Historical Society of Pennsylvania)

Landon, a banker by profession, became an independent petroleum producer and amassed a fortune. Elected governor in the Roosevelt landslide year in 1932, he was reelected in 1934, the only Republican governor to emerge unscathed that year. Landon supported many features of the New Deal, but he believed the programs could be run more efficiently and less expensively. He preached economy in government and balanced the Kansas budget. By consensus he was the Republican choice to run against FDR, even though he had to eliminate a challenge from Senator William Borah of Idaho, who had won a series of primaries. Herbert Hoover, still vigorous, toured the country and attempted to drum up support, but given his drubbing in 1932, the Republicans were looking for a fresh face. And so Landon looked like the best Republican to challenge FDR.

Pennsylvania Republicans still exerted influence at the national nominating convention. It took the Republicans but a single ballot at their June convention in Cleveland to nominate Landon with 984 votes to Borah's mere 19. There was also little debate over the vice presidential candidate. The Landon campaign wanted Senator Arthur H. Vandenberg of Michigan, but among others, the Pennsylvania delegation's desire for Chicago newspaper publisher Frank Knox ended the brief debate over the second spot, and Knox was nominated.[7]

As the national Democratic convention also approached in June, politics in Pennsylvania had reached a turning point. The development of genuine two-party competition was not just a test of FDR's personal popularity; it also would determine whether Democratic Governor George Earle would be able to implement his own "Little New Deal" programs. Despite the Democratic national sweep in 1932, Hoover had carried Pennsylvania and the Republican political machine was still very formidable. Importantly, the state Senate remained in Republican hands, which frustrated Earle's efforts to implement a state version of the New Deal. Earle's proposals included a series of state programs to provide relief for the unemployed and to have the state participate in the benefits of the national Social Security Act passed by Congress in 1935.[8]

President Franklin Roosevelt rides with Pennsylvania politicians Senator Joe Guffey and Governor George Earle to a campaign rally at the state capitol in Harrisburg days before the 1936 election. (Pennsylvania State Archives, MG-342, George Howard Earle Papers)

National Democratic leaders, cognizant of Earle's challenge and willing to help break the Republicans' stranglehold, chose Philadelphia as the site of their 1936 national convention. This was the first time one of the major parties had held its quadrennial meeting in Philadelphia since the Republicans met in 1900 to nominate the William McKinley-Theodore Roosevelt ticket.

Contrary to custom, the original offer for Philadelphia to host the Democratic convention came personally from the anti-New Deal Republican mayor, Samuel Davis Wilson. He offered the Democrats $200,000 to bring the convention to the city and then went on a crusade to be sure the hotel and restaurant owners did not gouge the attendees. Philadelphia truly spread a welcome mat for the delegates. The city even suspended its old Blue Laws and allowed conventioneers to imbibe alcohol on Sunday. Finally, in what must have been the most bizarre invitation in presidential convention history, the mayor offered cash prizes for the best essays written by the attending delegates dealing with the history and culture of Philadelphia. Who won what in the contest has never been discovered, but the *New York Times* on June 29 reported that the delegates spent a cool $1.5 million in Philadelphia.[9]

The Democrats renominated FDR and Vice President John Nance Garner by acclamation – with no debate or even a roll call vote. The liveliest moment was an hour-long demonstration the evening FDR was nominated in Convention Hall. The most memorable moment, however, was when FDR, in his acceptance delivered outdoors at the University of Pennsylvania's Franklin Field, took on the old moneyed powers in the country. Distressed over the criticism from his conservative critics, Roosevelt took off the gloves and declared that "during my first administration I would like to have it said they have met their match, of my second administration I would like to have it said they have met their master." FDR was giving no quarter in his fight against those he called the "royalists of the economic order."

Little happened at the convention that was otherwise noteworthy with the exception of the repeal of the infamous two-thirds rule, which required two-thirds majority votes for the nomination of presidential and vice presidential candidates. This rule had been in large part responsible for deadlocks at previous Democratic conventions.

As the host governor, Earle addressed the convention and rallied the faithful. But Earle did not rest there. He announced he would campaign in every county in the state, not once but three times between Labor Day and the election. His stump speech contained a very simple message. The election, he insisted, was about Roosevelt and the preservation of the New Deal. He vigorously argued for expanding its programs. Invigorated by the prospect of winning Pennsylvania, the Democrats barnstormed the state with their candidates and party leaders. No town, plant gate, or village square was too small for the caravan of Democratic orators. In October Roosevelt joined the tour. He reprised his speech at Forbes field, again to a standing-room-only crowd, delivering an appeal for a straight party vote.

The Republicans were not prepared to surrender a state in which the electoral vote had been delivered for every Republican candidate since Lincoln's first presidential victory in 1860. They campaigned hard, fully understanding the stakes. They also resorted to excessive rhetoric, arguing that the Democratic Party had been taken over by communists and socialists. Befitting the bitterness of the campaign, the Republican commissioners of rural Potter County locked the Democratic governor out of the court house when he showed up to campaign for his party's candidates, despite a long-honored tradition of allowing both parties to use the venue for such speeches.[10]

Pennsylvania Republicans also got some help from one prominent Democrat, the 1928 presidential candidate Al Smith, who had broken with FDR over the expansion of the federal government under the New Deal. Campaigning in Philadelphia, Smith ripped FDR for abandoning the conservative 1932 Democratic platform. But he did not limit his attacks to the president and the New Deal. He went after Earle, contending that the governor brought about "anarchy" by allowing coal to be mined in the state illegally. He even went as far as to suggest that Earle be impeached. Earle responded by calling Smith a treasonous Benedict Arnold for failing to support FDR.

Earle's efforts on the campaign circuit in 1936 and his strong support of the New Deal did not go unnoticed nationally. Though only 45 when elected governor in 1934, and despite a reputation for impulsiveness and volatility, he was touted by some in the national press corps as a possible presidential nominee should FDR not seek a third term.

In addition to the customary candidate rallies and speeches, a Pennsylvania political leader introduced a campaign innovation. In 1934 in the Pennsylvania campaign for governor, Matt McCloskey, a contractor and major Democratic fundraiser, held a $100-per-plate dinner in Montgomery County. Only a dozen people showed up and paid the $100. But in the 1936 presidential campaign, McCloskey held a similar dinner for Roosevelt at the Penn Athletic Club in Philadelphia, and nearly 1,900 folks paid. With this success, both parties began to hold these events routinely and a fundraising innovation was born.

The results of the national general election were a foregone conclusion. FDR was overwhelmingly reelected, 27.5 million to Landon's 16.7 million. The electoral vote was an astonishing 523 votes for Roosevelt, 8 votes for Landon. Only Maine and Vermont went for Landon. A third party, the Union Party, composed of an amalgam of left-wing dissidents, could only manage 882,000 votes. The

Democrats increased their already substantial majorities in the Congress; the Republicans started the new Congress in 1937 with only sixteen senators and eighty-nine House members.

In Pennsylvania, FDR won forty-one counties; the Democrats would not win this many counties again. Republican counties fell like dominoes, including Philadelphia, Bucks, Lebanon, Dauphin, Carbon, Armstrong, Perry, and Cumberland. Roosevelt won Philadelphia by a remarkable 209,000 votes, sweeping forty-three of the fifty wards. Furthermore, the Democrats reinforced the allegiance of voters from blue-collar, Catholic, union families in the industrial counties of Fayette, Greene, Washington, Westmoreland, and Lackawanna. Landon's twenty-six counties were mostly rural, forest or farming areas. Overall FDR won 57 percent of the vote in the state; Landon won 41 percent, and consequently the Democrats captured the state's 36 electoral votes for the first time in eighty years. Republicans naturally were stunned, perhaps no one more than Republican political boss Joe Grundy, who instructed the editor of his newspaper, the *Doylestown Intelligencer*, to print the news story of FDR's victory on the back page of the paper.

The 1936 election solidified the resurgence of the national Democratic Party, and it made permanent the coalition of voters that transformed the Democrats into the majority party for the first time since before the Civil War. In Pennsylvania, the FDR landslide translated into a Democratic statewide sweep; the party won the state House and Senate and two statewide offices as well. In addition to the ethnic Catholics, many of whom lived in the southwestern part of the state and in various wards of Philadelphia, the new Democratic coalition consisted of two other important elements. One group was organized labor, which had benefited from the passage of New Deal employment and labor laws. The United Mine Workers membership, for example, went from 60,000 in 1932 to 500,000 in 1936. Other unions' membership rose as well. The Democrats assiduously courted labor leaders, and they responded with a vigorous outpouring of workers for the Democrats. Another group was black voters, who pivoted to Roosevelt in large numbers. Blacks had started the drift to the Democrats in 1932, but the pace of the shift in 1936 was impressive. The black Democratic vote increased by about 20 percent in Philadelphia and the Democrats for the first time in history won a majority in those wards and divisions where blacks were a majority. The movement of black voters into the Democratic Party would not be complete, however, until the final conversion took place in Philadelphia in the 1950s.[11]

Chapter 2
The Republicans Revitalize: the 1940s

The 1940s saw a return of Republican dominance in Pennsylvania, albeit more narrowly than before the realignment of the 1930s. After the Republicans captured the governorship in 1938, they reversed their New Deal losses. The Democrats in the 1940s actually saw their voter registration fall below 40 percent of the two-party total. When FDR headed the tickets in 1940 and 1944, the party still won some state elections. Joseph Guffey won reelection to the Senate in 1940; Francis J. Myers scored a surprising victory in the contest for the other U.S. Senate seat in 1944, and Democrats won a few other statewide offices. These victories were reversed when both senators were followed by Republicans: Edward Martin in 1946 and James H. Duff in 1950. The governorship, together with the considerable patronage that accrued to the office, slipped back into Republicans hands.

1940: Roosevelt and Willkie

The years of FDR's second term opened possibilities for the Republicans nationally as well as in Pennsylvania. The nation still had not recovered from the Great Depression and had even slipped into recession in 1937 as FDR cut back on New Deal spending in an attempt to balance the budget. The president had three additional problems that posed political challenges: his unsuccessful attempt to increase the number of justices on the Supreme Court; the outbreak of war in Europe and the debate over military preparedness; and finally, questions over how the nation would react to his candidacy for a third term.

Through most of the second term, no clear favorite emerged among the Republicans to challenge Roosevelt. The Republicans held their national convention in Philadelphia, perhaps to rekindle support in a city they had politically owned since the Civil War but had lost to FDR in 1936. The Republicans still controlled City Hall, and they were not prepared to surrender it or the state without a fight. The June 24 Republican convention opened to great fanfare. The Mummers strutted, and the party's ancient but still active former President Herbert Hoover addressed a rally at Independence Hall.

Three names were most commonly mentioned as likely presidential nominees as convention time drew near: Thomas E. Dewey, the district attorney of New York; Ohio Senator Robert A. Taft, a conservative and a staunch isolationist; and Michigan's veteran Senator Arthur H. Vandenberg. But a host of favorite sons also appeared as possibilities. Among them was Pennsylvania Governor Arthur H. James, whose name was placed in nomination. James, a former lieutenant governor and superior court judge, was a product of the Luzerne County Republican organization. His candidacy in 1940 was orchestrated by the reigning Republican political boss, Sun Oil magnate Joseph Pew, perhaps more to hold the Republican delegation together for bargaining purposes.[12]

Despite being a life-long Republican, Pew had endorsed FDR in 1932. His support for the New Deal disappeared, however, as soon as the president proposed price controls on oil. For Pew, a Philadelphia based-oil man, this was a "wicked idea" as antithetical to free enterprise as the trusts of the late nineteenth century. Thereafter, Pew dedicated his life to the defeat of the New Deal and the success of the Republican Party. By 1940, Pew had become the de facto head of the Republican Party in the state and a major national player as well. By 1940, he and family members had contributed $2 million to the party. Pew was a controversial figure, however. To his enemies, he was a reactionary millionaire attempting to buy his brand of government. By contrast, Pew viewed himself as a contemporary Revolutionary patriot, saving the foundations of American government.[13]

In 1940, President Franklin Roosevelt's decision to seek an unprecedented third term drew criticism from many quarters. Here, Pennsylvania supporters of his opponent, Wendell Willkie, use the figure of Uncle Sam to protest Roosevelt's third-term ambitions as undemocratic. (Temple University Libraries, Urban Archives)

James's election to the governorship in 1938 began sixteen years of Republican control of the office. The Pennsylvania convention delegation was overwhelmingly committed to him, but notably, future Pennsylvania congressman and U.S. Senator Hugh D. Scott was not. Early on Scott had decided to work for long-shot Wendell Willkie, who was not a serious contender at the outset of the presidential contest. Willkie had been a Democrat and a supporter of FDR in 1932, but he left the party over the New Deal's expansion of the federal government and regulation. As a lawyer for an energy company, the Commonwealth and Southern, Willkie became embroiled in a legal dispute with the Tennessee Valley Authority that brought him national attention. A national speaking tour against the New Deal led to the formation of almost five hundred Willkie clubs. His rise from political obscurity to national prominence was meteoric. His outspoken internationalism put him at odds with the majority of his party's committed isolationist leaders. Articulate, savvy, and energetic, he amazingly pulled into second place in the American Institute of Public Opinion Poll taken on the eve of the Philadelphia convention.

The other candidates did not sit idly. Tom Dewey, who made a national reputation as a crime-fighting district attorney in New York City with spectacular indictments and prosecutions, was the most energetic of the candidates. He began a national speaking tour himself, chalking up 25,000 travel miles and entering the primaries. He won Wisconsin and Nebraska, and by the opening of the convention he had about 40 percent of the delegates committed to him. Taft, working through the Republican establishment, went into the convention with about 20 percent of the total vote while Vandenberg's candidacy collapsed.

Willkie's opponents refused to believe he could win the nomination and therefore did not form a coalition to stop his momentum. Additionally, Willkie was helped by the rapid success of the Germans sweeping through Western Europe during the first months of 1940, which changed many Americans' positions on aiding the Allies. From the opening gavel of the convention, telegrams and public opinion pressured the delegates to vote for Willkie, whose campaign had generated incredible grassroots Republican support. The Republican convention was held in Philadelphia, and within the walls of Convention Hall, "We want Willkie" chants echoed from the packed galleries. The first and second ballots were indecisive, however. On the first ballot, Dewey led with 360 votes followed by Taft with 189 and Willkie in third with 105. Pennsylvania Governor James had 74 votes as Pennsylvania held firm for its favorite son.

Willkie had a very serious problem with Joe Pew. The Pennsylvania political boss disliked Willkie, and the differences were more than just philosophical. Willkie considered Pew a throw-back to the Dark Ages, an old reactionary political boss who prevented the party from evolving into a formidable opponent to FDR's New Deal programs. Pew thought the utility executive was a phony

Dressed as mine workers, a group of men express their support for Pennsylvania governor Arthur H. James at the Republican National Convention in 1940. While the state delegation initially held firm in favor of its favorite son, all of Pennsylvania's delegates ultimately went to the party's eventual nominee, Wendell Willkie. (Temple University Libraries, Urban Archives)

Republican and a belated transplant to the Republican Party. He never trusted Willkie's anti-New Dealism. Between the second and third ballots Willkie was advised that, despite the differences between the two, Pew might be willing to negotiate Pennsylvania's 72 convention votes, but the future nominee rejected any deals, believing he could win the nomination without the votes of the Keystone State. On the third ballot Willkie moved into second place behind Dewey. Ten Pennsylvania votes were cast for Willkie, but Pew was not willing to release the entire delegation. When told of Pew's refusal, he relied tartly, "Pew be damned." Willkie was nominated on the sixth ballot with 998 votes, even as ballots were being changed as the roll call progressed. As journalist Dan Rottenberg relates the story, Pew's butler refused to get him out of his bath in his Ardmore home when the request came to release the Pennsylvania delegation. But it mattered little what Pew did. The Pennsylvania votes were unanimously cast for Willkie in the end. And Pew reluctantly supported him after the nomination.[14]

Early in 1940, FDR was still uncommitted to a third term. But numerous party leaders worked diligently toward that end. In Pennsylvania, the effort was led by Governor George Earle. In December 1939, he issued a statement saying that it should be left to Roosevelt to explain his record, obviously making the point that the voters should decide whether the two-term precedent should continue. He made it clear that he thought FDR would carry the state for a third term, and he left no doubt that the state's delegation to the Democratic convention would be for the president. The next year Earle wrote about FDR's record in a book not surprisingly titled *Roosevelt Again*. In it, he attempted to debunk the idea of the third term limitation. With 50,000 copies disseminated around the country, the volume helped set the stage for the great national debate over a Roosevelt third term. Earle naturally sent Roosevelt a copy and received a courteous response, but the president refused to indicate whether he actively would seek the third term.[15]

Roosevelt remained evasive, but he was willing to accept the nomination if a genuine draft took place. No logical successor was immediately apparent. Several members of his administration, a few senators, and Vice President Garner wanted the nomination; Pennsylvania's George Earle was also mentioned as a possibility. Given the circumstances, FDR permitted his vice president and his postmaster general, Jim Farley, to enter primaries in which FDR was also on the ballot. The president coasted to easy victories against them.

Despite a lack of clarity at the July Chicago convention about Roosevelt's true intentions to run for a third term, he was easily and overwhelmingly renominated. The most suspense at the convention centered on the selection of a running mate for Roosevelt, a matter that once again found Pennsylvanians exerting influence. Garner was out of the picture; he had wanted the presidential nomination for himself, which made him unacceptable to Roosevelt. A number of Democrats were interested, notably a group of U.S. senators and several members of

Roosevelt's cabinet. Although Pennsylvania party leader David Lawrence's personal favorite was Paul V. McNutt, the governor of Indiana, he delivered 68 of the state's 73 delegate votes for Roosevelt's choice, Secretary of Agriculture Henry A. Wallace. During a personal meeting with the president prior to the convention, Lawrence had learned that FDR wanted Wallace on the ticket to beef up Democratic support in the Midwest farm belt.[16]

The fall campaign was set against the backdrop of the expanding war in Europe. By election time, the Battle of Britain had taken place, the lend-lease deal that sent fifty old American destroyers to England in exchange for long-term base leases had been announced, and FDR had convinced Congress to approve the first peacetime draft. Willkie, to the dismay of many of his party's isolationist leaders, endorsed these proposals at first before shifting positions and going on the attack by accusing FDR of taking the county to war.

In Pennsylvania, the personal and philosophical differences between Willkie and Pew grew into an internecine struggle among the Willkie campaign, its volunteers, and the party's conservative establishment and political leaders. The nominee, a virtual outsider who had never held political office, refused to allow the Republican National Committee to direct the campaign, which led to conflict at all levels of party organization. The situation reached the theater of the absurd when Willkie supporters in Pittsburgh refused to let Governor James anywhere near the presidential candidate when he campaigned in the city. But the most serious problem for the Republicans existed in Philadelphia. There the Willkie volunteers, through the Willkie Clubs, moved to take over the party at the division level, prompting fear that party regulars would lose control of the patronage. The situation deteriorated to the point that Willkie met with Pew in early October to end the feud and find a way to blend the two organizations into an effective campaign force. Tensions continued, and a Gallup Poll late in the campaign showing a likely FDR victory in the city further demoralized the Republicans. Sensing they would lose the presidency, Republican leaders in Philadelphia directed the lion's share of their efforts to holding onto state and congressional offices.[17]

Although few doubted that FDR would prevail, he did less well in the national popular vote in 1940 than in 1936. He won 55 percent to 45 percent. Willkie managed to win five million more votes than Landon had won in 1936. Willkie won only ten states to FDR's thirty-eight and in the vote that counted, the electoral vote, the race was similarly one-sided. FDR won 449 to Willkie's 82 votes.

In Pennsylvania, the election produced a Roosevelt victory, but as in the national tabulation, the election was much closer than four years earlier. FDR won 53 percent to 46 percent, a four-point decline from 1936, and Willkie improved his party's performance by five points. Similarly, the president could not match his 1936 county performance. He had won forty-one counties in 1936, but that number dropped to twenty-five in 1940. He did win Philadelphia by 177,000 votes and Allegheny by 105,000. The core Democratic counties in the southwest and the northeast stayed with the president.

1944: Roosevelt and Dewey

The Japanese attack on Pearl Harbor on December 7, 1941, ended the isolationist debate in the country as the war effort came to dominate politics in the nation. The country fought a war on two fronts in Europe and the Pacific. As FDR aptly put it, "Dr. New Deal" gave way to "Dr. Win the War." Faced with the spending realities imposed by the war, the federal budget ballooned between 1939 and 1945 from $9 billon to $100 billon. As conservatives gained in Congress, Roosevelt dropped some of the New Deal programs, including the Works Progress Administration, the Civilian Conservation Corps, and the National Youth Administration. Republicans had picked up forty-six seats in the House and nine in the Senate in 1942.

In the midst of the war, FDR had no real Democratic opposition on his way to a fourth-term nomination. National polls showed that Democrats wanted him to seek another term, and that he most likely would win reelection. The president was somewhat coy about the fourth term, but his decision to run again was taken for granted and Pennsylvania's Democratic leaders stood rock-solid in support. Led by David Lawrence and Emma Guffey Miller, the sister of Senator Joseph Guffey and a national committeewoman, party leaders lined up early behind a Roosevelt fourth term. The obvious harmony resulted in a low primary turnout. About 320,000 Democrats voted for FDR, a decline of almost 50 percent from the 1940 primary.

At the Democratic National Convention in Chicago in July, persistent concerns about the president's health led to a battle over the vice presidential nomination and Pennsylvanians joined in the wrangling. Some national party leaders and conservative southerners, thinking it possible that Roosevelt might not live through another full term, wanted the liberal Vice President Wallace removed from the ticket. The president, wanting to avoid a costly internal fight, agreed to replace Wallace with Senator Harry S. Truman of Missouri. The Pennsylvania delegation was deeply divided. Lawrence, along with Allegheny County Commissioner John Kane, backed Truman; the Guffeys, brother and sister, and CIO President Philip Murray ardently supported Wallace. The Guffey faction distrusted Truman because of his relationship with Kansas political boss Tom Pendergast, then jailed for public corruption. But Lawrence, who had campaigned with Truman in Pittsburgh and York earlier in 1944, personally liked the Missouri senator. Pennsylvania's divided delegation showed when Truman was nominated on the second ballot, but he received only 24 of the state's 72 convention votes.

Only after Truman had more than the necessary votes for nomination did Guffey move to make the result unanimous.[18]

The Republicans became more encouraged about defeating FDR over the course of the 1944 campaign season. The gains made in the midterm elections and the war weariness factor gave Republicans an enthusiasm they had not had since 1928. Also, Pennsylvania and seven other large, mostly industrial states had Republican governors, and they represented a huge bloc of 207 electoral votes. Powerful Republican leaders, including Pennsylvania's Joseph Pew, opposed nominating Wendell Willkie again and turned instead to Thomas E. Dewey, the recently elected governor of New York. But by the time of the June convention, Dewey was not even a formally announced candidate, and his positions on national issues were only vaguely understood by the delegates. He was thought to be mildly inter-

Potential voters observe a voting machine demonstration at Philadelphia's 30th Street station prior to the 1944 presidential election. (Temple University Libraries, Urban Archives)

nationalist and moderately liberal. Notwithstanding the vagueness of his positions, the convention nominated him easily.

The fall campaign was not particularly memorable. The Republicans focused on FDR's health and the cost and inefficiencies of the New Deal. They also tried to make the argument that FDR was too closely tied to labor unions, which Republicans alleged to be under communist influence. Supporting this argument, the *Philadelphia Inquirer* asserted in an editorial that a vote for Dewey was a vote against the growing power of communism in the nation.[19]

By the end of October, FDR appeared more robust and began a swing from New York to Pennsylvania and then to the Midwest. On October 24, he spent four hours in Philadelphia, campaigning in an open car despite a drizzle and brutal wind. In an evening address, he reminded an enthusiastic crowd of the nation's military successes; fortunately for him, General Douglas MacArthur had made his victorious landing in the Philippines just four days before. For the balance of the campaign, FDR touted recent military victories.[20]

In Pennsylvania and the nation, the election results were predictable: a Democratic victory. Following in Willkie's path, Dewey continued to erode FDR's majority. Nationally, the popular-vote victory by the president was just under eight percentage points, the smallest of his four elections, 54 percent to 46 percent. He still easily secured a majority of the electoral vote, 432 to 99, limiting Dewey to winning only twelve of the forty-eight states.

FDR narrowly won Pennsylvania, with 51 percent to his opponent's 48 percent. Roosevelt slipped two percentage points from his performance in 1940 while Dewey gained two percentage points over Willkie's showing. The president's 1.9 million votes were 231,000 fewer than he had won in 1940. He won only sixteen counties, a drop of twenty-five from his high of forty-one in 1936. He still won the big urban centers, which gave him votes essential for his victory. His margin over Dewey statewide was 105,000 votes, but he won Philadelphia by almost 150,000 votes. Turnout was 60 percent of eligible voters, down 13 points from 1936, and the Democrats fared more poorly in the rural parts of the state than in 1940. Without the popular Roosevelt on the national ticket in future elections, the fortunes of the Democrats would change markedly.

1948: Truman and Dewey

At the beginning of 1948, few observers believed that President Truman was likely to win election to a full term. Truman had assumed the presidency after Roosevelt's death on April 12, 1945. As often is the case, the American public warmly welcomed the new president. His approval rating as measured by a Gallup poll pushed 90 percent, but within a year it dropped to the low thirties. What happened? Truman was handed two serious and growing problems, one a worsening economy and the second the expanding complexities of the Cold War.

On the domestic front, when Truman vetoed a bill that would have continued price controls that had been in effect during World War II, the resulting inflation fueled demands from unions that wages be raised. That in turn led to strikes in major sectors of the economy – steel, coal, and automobiles. The new president twice ordered government seizures of the mines. Reacting abruptly and quickly in

President Harry Truman takes in the Liberty Bell during a campaign tour through Philadelphia in 1948. (Temple University Libraries, Urban Archives)

the face of a national railway engineer's strike, Truman seized the rail system. Angry at the president's action, a large number of labor unions deserted the Democrats in the 1946 midterm election, despite Truman's persistent opposition to the Taft-Hartley Act, a law to restrict labor union powers and activities, which Congress later passed over his veto. With an economic slump in place, the Republicans captured both houses of Congress for the first time since 1938. The new Republican Congress made mincemeat of Truman's domestic proposals.

Given this set of circumstances, a united Republican Party seemed likely to win back the presidency for the first time in twenty years. Sensing victory, Republicans had a bevy of possible nominees early in the year. Some favorite sons from 1944, including California Governor Earl Warren and former Minnesota Governor Harold E. Stassen, were under consideration, but the major contenders were the 1944 nominee Thomas Dewey and Senator Robert Taft from Ohio. The conservative Taft, one of the party's leading isolationists, was considered Dewey's most important rival. However, Stassen, the most liberal of the Republicans (and later president of the University of Pennsylvania), won a series of primaries in the early months of 1948. This forced Dewey to abandon his strategy of staying quietly in New York and campaign actively for the nomination.

Going into the April 27 Pennsylvania primary, the state's Republican leaders remained divided on the choice of a nominee. Some stood behind a favorite son, U.S. Senator Edward Martin of Greene County, a former governor elected to the Senate in 1946 in a huge victory by more than 600,000 votes. No one expected Martin to become the nominee, and his status as favorite son only nominally held the divided delegation together. But Martin insisted he would remain in the contest until the end. Meanwhile, Stassen continued his momentum. In a primary in which voters were required to write in their choice for president, Stassen secured approximately 74,000 votes, Dewey 68,000, and Martin 42,000. More importantly, though, this vote did not bind the delegates to these presidential preferences, creating fluidity within the delegation.

In a surprising series of decisions, the two major parties and the Progressive Party all decided to hold their 1948 nomination conventions in Philadelphia. The Republicans arrived first, in June. Tickets for the 15,000-seat Convention Hall were hard to find. Republicans were ecstatic, believing victory was at hand. The Republicans partied well into the wee hours of the morning, and the enthusiasm extended into the streets of the city.

Neither Martin's favorite-son status nor the primary results halted the political machinations within the state Republican leadership. Governor Duff made an all-out effort to stop Dewey, and in so doing he took on his party's political bosses, especially the head of the powerful Pennsylvania Manufacturers' Association, Joseph Grundy. Duff knew Dewey personally and believed others, such as Senator Arthur Vandenberg or General Dwight Eisenhower, were more

Campaign workers for 1948 Republican candidate Thomas E. Dewey strike a pose of support at his Philadelphia campaign headquarters before taking their cause to the streets. (Temple University Libraries, Urban Archives)

qualified. But when neither of them entered the race, he was left without a candidate. His fall-back choice was Taft, and Duff worked diligently for him at the convention. The effort was in vain, however. Ultimately, Martin's lieutenants made a deal to throw Pennsylvania's support to Dewey for the honorific and patronage rewards that customarily attended nomination deal-making. The state was awarded the honor of placing Dewey's name in nomination for president, and Martin and Joe Grundy were promised control over the 10,000 federal patronage jobs in the state. As a sweetener, three-term congressman Hugh Scott was promised the chairmanship of the National Republican Party.[21]

　　　The Democrats in 1948 faced defections from both their right and left wings. On the right, southern Democrats bolted the national convention when liberals successfully passed a pro-civil rights, pro-labor platform. Furious over what they perceived as their party's commitment to use the federal government to regulate race relations, some southern Democratic leaders formed the States Rights or Dixiecrat Party. Their presidential nominee was Governor Strom Thurmond of South Carolina, a devoted segregationist.

On the left, the dissidents nominated Henry Wallace, whom Truman had fired from his cabinet. Running under the Progressive Party banner, Wallace and his supporters wanted more cooperation with the Soviet Union and greater federal powers over the direction of the economy. Wallace was neither a communist nor a sympathizer, but he was very ineffective in defending himself against these charges as he continued to argue for more cooperation with the Soviets.

The two major party conventions could not have provided more contrast. The Democratic convention reminded observers of a funeral gathering, or to paraphrase *Time*, the convention was a wake before an election funeral. Conventioneers were listless and uninspired. Complaints were common in the city as scores of hotel and restaurant cancellations were reported, and the managers of the convention literally had people standing on street corners inviting the public to attend the sessions. Defeat was in the air.[22]

Since the convention was held in a Republican city, the welcoming address was given by David Lawrence, by now the mayor of Pittsburgh. According to observers, Lawrence's speech attacking the Republican Congress and reigning Republican political boss Joseph Pew was less than exciting. One Pennsylvania participant declared the convention depressing, and others were quick to note the lack of enthusiasm and the general inattentiveness of the delegates.[23]

Probably a majority of Democratic delegates came to Philadelphia determined to nominate someone other than Truman. A liberal faction led by a new organization, Americans for Democratic Action (ADA), was the most organized. The Philadelphia chapter had a strong contingent of local members prepared to help find an alternative. Truman's opponents really had no strong challenger to put forward, but they waged a floor fight over the platform and pushed the party to adopt a strong civil rights plank. The plank moved beyond the party's very general 1944 statement, which held that racial and religious minorities had the right to live, work, and vote equally with all citizens but left enforcement of these matters to the states. Southern delegates had little objection to such a vague plank, but the new statement pushed by the ADA was specific about the extension of these rights. The Pennsylvania delegation voted in favor of the stronger civil rights plank. Some southern delegates walked out of the convention and the Dixiecrat Party emerged out of their desertion.

Without a viable opponent Truman won nomination on the first ballot. He was aided immensely by Lawrence, who gathered support among the party's big-city leaders. Truman's nomination did not exactly fill Lawrence and other Pennsylvania Democrats with confidence that they would win the election. But in an otherwise mundane speech to the delegates, Truman surprised everyone when he called for a special session of Congress, beginning on July 26, to take up an aggressive agenda dealing with housing, agriculture, civil rights, and other domestic matters. As a call for action, Truman's bold move had major consequences on the outcome of the election.

Convention Hall was barely vacated and cleaned when the Progressives took over the venue. Unfortunately for the party nominee, Henry Wallace, his party's convention was hijacked by a pro-Communist faction that dictated a party platform articulating a pro-Soviet foreign policy. Moving the party farther to the left, this pretty much sank the Wallace campaign.

As Labor Day approached, the campaigns began in earnest. Many historians still marvel that with a fractured party Truman was able to win the 1948 election. His campaign ranks as one of the most remarkable comebacks in American history. He did it in part with the strategy of calling the Congress back into session in July and challenging the Republicans, controlling both Houses, to enact their own convention platform into law. When they did not, Truman began an amazing cross-county speaking tour in which he berated the "the do-nothing Republican Congress" – a reference that reverberated throughout the nation. As the campaign progressed, the major elements of the Democratic coalition came home. Labor realized that workers would fare better under Truman than the Republicans, and some farmers returned to Truman because Republicans would not support full-parity price supports. Liberal and Jewish voters also moved to Truman after his recognition of Israel earlier in the year.

A self-confident Dewey ran a somewhat lackadaisical and unfocused campaign, expecting an easy victory. The election results stunned the nation. In what has become one of the most famous political photographs, a jubilant Truman was shown holding a copy of the *Chicago Tribune* with the banner headline reading, "Dewey Defeats Truman." Truman's victory was nonetheless a squeaker; he won 50 percent of the popular vote to Dewey's 45 percent. His electoral vote was convincing, 303 to 189, or 57 percent to 36 percent. As expected, Thurmond carried five states, four of them southern, for 39 electoral votes, but Wallace did not win a single state.

More than 3.7 million Pennsylvanians voted, and Dewey just barely edged out Truman by 51 percent to 47 percent, or by 150,000 votes. Collectively, five third-party candidates managed only 2 percent of the vote. Wallace barely topped 55,000. Truman only carried thirteen of the sixty-seven counties, but importantly for the Democrats in later elections, he won Philadelphia by a two-to-one margin. The remainder of the Truman plurality came from the traditional Democratic strongholds in the southwest: Allegheny, Beaver, Cambria, Fayette, Greene, Washington, and Westmoreland, and a smattering of others around the state, Lackawanna, Northampton, Elk, York, and Berks.

Nationally, the Democrats had won a string of five straight presidential elections –something the party had not been able to do since its inception in 1828. In Pennsylvania, however, the Democratic Party's string of victories had been halted at three. The party would not carry the state in a presidential election again until the razor-thin victory of John F. Kennedy in 1960.

Citizens lining up to vote at a Philadelphia polling place in 1948 exemplify the New Deal coalition brought together under President Franklin Roosevelt during the 1930s and 40s. With the help of this coalition, Democrats achieved electoral success in traditionally Republican Pennsylvania, a transition that they hoped to continue past Roosevelt's presidency. (Temple University Libraries, Urban Archives)

Chapter 3

The Transitional Decade: the 1950s

Only the personal popularity of Dwight D. Eisenhower, a World War II hero, and the unpopularity of the Korean War were capable of breaking the Democrats' grip on the presidency. For Democrats in Pennsylvania, the picture was more complex, however. The 1950s were a transitional decade in the politics of the state. The evolution of Pennsylvania into a genuinely competitive two-party state had begun with the New Deal, especially the conversion of Pittsburgh into a Democratic stronghold. When reform Democrats took over Philadelphia in 1951, the party finally had the votes necessary to make the state competitive.

Another important factor in the rise of two-party competition was the conversion of black voters from the Republican to the Democratic Party, a process underway since the 1930s. In Philadelphia, the policies of reform Democratic mayors Joseph S. Clark and Richardson Dilworth during the 1950s accelerated the pace. In the 1952 presidential election and thereafter, African Americans in the seventeen wards in Philadelphia with sizable black populations gave huge percentages of their votes to Democratic candidates: 68 percent in 1952, 68 percent in 1956, and 78 percent in 1960. By the end of decade, Philadelphia blacks comprised about one-fifth or about 200,000 of the city's registered voters, and four-fifths of them could now be counted on to vote consistently for the Democratic ticket. The situation in the rest of the southeast was more complex. While a majority of black voters would on occasion support a Democratic presidential ticket, the counties in the southeast remained dominated by aging Republican warlords. They consistently returned large black majorities for Republican candidates in local and state elections.[24]

In geographic terms, the Republicans dominated two-thirds of Pennsylvania's sixty-seven counties, most of them rural and suburban, while Democrats controlled the more populous urban counties. This meant that from the 1950s forward, most elections would be close and competitive. In addition to the changing demographics of their party, the Democrats were helped by a series of internal fights within the Republican Party and by their own new and more vigorous leadership.

1952: Eisenhower and Stevenson

By 1952, the Truman administration had become shrouded in controversy. Buffeted by scandal within his administration and the stalemate in ending the Korean War, the president's approval rating shrank below 30 percent, an all-time low for him. The big question confronting the Democrats in 1952 was whether Truman would run again. No sooner did he take himself out of the race in March than a large number of contenders emerged. The most serious of them were Vice President Alben W. Barkley, Senator C. Estes Kefauver of Tennessee, and Governor Adlai E. Stevenson of Illinois. Stevenson was not exactly enthusiastic about making the race, but many Democratic leaders pressured him to run.

Democrats in Pennsylvania were not united in support for any of the possible nominees. A group of Philadelphia liberals, led by Mayor Joe Clark and then-Controller Richardson Dilworth, were for Kefauver, best known for his Senate investigations of racketeering and organized crime. Although many of Clark's political associates favored Stevenson, Clark and the liberals questioned the Illinois governor's commitment to civil rights. Simply put, they believed Stevenson did not support federal action to expand those rights. But the liberals also supported Kefauver because he would be the "unbossed" candidate, independent of the party's political leaders and more the candidate of the party's grassroots. Prior to the Democratic convention, Kefauver courted Clark's support by sending two books he had written, *Crime in America* and *Twentieth Century Congress.* Clark promised to get a letter out to the Pennsylvania convention delegation on Kefauver's behalf, but more importantly Kefauver importuned Clark to form a "mayors for Kefauver" organization to promote his candidacy.

In Pittsburgh, Mayor David Lawrence was publicly neutral, but he told Fayette County Democrats in early June that he expected Stevenson to become the nominee. At the end of June, in a private meeting in Philadelphia with a handful of party leaders, he was antagonistic to Kefauver and insisted the senator could not win. At the national convention in Chicago, Lawrence made it clear he was for Stevenson when he convened the state delegation, and he called a surprise caucus just prior to the opening of the session. In the caucus, he voted first and vocally called out Stevenson's name, thereby influencing the straw vote that cast 32 votes for Stevenson and 15.5 votes for Kefauver, with the remainder going elsewhere. This maneuver outraged the Kefauver supporters. Complicated politics and negotiations ensued with Lawrence in the thick of the politicking until Stevenson won the nomination on the third ballot. Pennsylvania eventually cast all of its 70 votes on behalf of the Illinois governor as the other candidacies collapsed. After the convention, the Democratic Party had no problem with unity. Kefauver pledged his active support for Stevenson, and the South was mollified with the addition of a southerner, Senator John J. Sparkman of Alabama, to the ticket as Stevenson's running mate. In Pennsylvania, the liberals happily swung to Stevenson and Clark became co-chairman of Stevenson's Pennsylvania campaign.[25]

The Republican nomination boiled down to a contest between General Dwight David Eisenhower and, once again, Ohio Senator Robert Taft. Nationally, Eisenhower was a very popular choice among the voters of both parties. He had been sought after by Republican and Democratic leaders to be their presidential standard bearer. His route to the presidency was that of many who had occupied the White House: war hero, not politician. Ike had led the Allied forces in Europe to victory over the Axis powers during World War II; he was then promoted to Army Chief of Staff. After a brief stint as the President of Columbia University, he became the first supreme commander of NATO (the North Atlantic Treaty Organization).

The general had substantial connections to Pennsylvania. His grandfather, Jacob, was a Mennonite minister and farmer who had lived in south-central Pennsylvania in the nineteenth century. He moved his family to Abilene, Kansas,

Female members of "Americans for Eisenhower" express their support for the Republican candidate before his 1952 campaign appearance at Independence Hall. (Temple University Libraries, Urban Archives)

after the Civil War. Ike's youngest brother, Milton, was president of Penn State from 1950 to 1956. A close confidante, he later became presidential adviser to his brother. In 1950, Ike purchased a farm in Gettysburg, which made him a resident of the state during the campaign in 1952, and after his service as president he retired to the farm.

It's not often that a Pennsylvania governor gets to be on the cover of *Time*, much less with a story titled "President Maker?" But that's exactly what happened to Republican Governor John S. Fine on the eve of the July 7 opening of the Republican National Convention. He was featured in *Time* because he faced one of the most critical decisions of his political career. Born in Luzerne County, Fine was the son of a coal miner but he decided on a different future. He graduated valedictorian of his high school class, skipped college, and went directly to Dickinson Law School. Returning to Luzerne, he became chairman of the Republican Party and eventually operated one of the most efficient, patronage-ridden organizations in the state. He was elected to two terms as a county judge and served on the state Superior Court before capturing the governorship in 1950.

Fine's position as putative kingmaker in the Chicago convention in 1952 was worlds apart from the coal fields of northeastern Pennsylvania. The kingmaker role came from the general acceptance that Fine controlled thirty votes in the state's seventy-member delegation. Whichever way Fine delivered the votes might well decide the tight nomination struggle between Eisenhower and Taft. Consequently, the governor came under close scrutiny by the national press. He was also under considerable pressure from an opposing faction in the state, headed by Senator Jim Duff, to back Ike. Duff and his Pennsylvania colleague, Senator Hugh Scott, both had been part of the first draft-Ike meeting among Republican national leaders in 1951. They were known as "Eastern Republicans," meaning internationalists in foreign policy with a special commitment to maintaining a close relationship and an American presence in Europe.[26]

As convention time approached the Pennsylvania delegation remained divided between Taft and Eisenhower. The best estimates were that about twenty-two delegates favored the general, eighteen were for Taft, and thirty who were uncommitted were with Fine, setting up the kingmaker role for the governor. The leaders might have been divided, but the Republican voters were not. In the spring Pennsylvania primary they had cast 863,758 votes for Eisenhower to only 178,629 for Taft in the preference vote, which was not binding on the elected delegates. Two other candidates were even less relevant: Harold Stassen ran a distant third with 120,305, and General Douglas MacArthur managed only 6,028.[27]

The Republican popular vote in the state did not move Fine, who refused to budge from his stance of neutrality. Right up to the Chicago convention, he rebuffed every effort to force his hand and publicly state a preference. At the convention he still remained mum. At one point in a credentials fight, he asked for but could not get a recess to caucus with the state's delegation. He flew into a rage at his failure to obtain the recess, and, with drool dripping from his mouth, the rage was caught on television. This spectacle brought Fine's role as kingmaker to an abrupt end. As journalist Paul Beers reported, when the nomination roll call was about to take place, the governor was absent from the hall, having the second of two Scotches with Clare Booth Luce. He rejoined the convention for the nomination vote; at last he wanted to deliver the delegation to Ike. He wanted to play the kingmaker role at a critical junction in the vote count by delivering the majority for Ike on the roll call vote. Pennsylvania had just cast 53 votes for Eisenhower and 15 for Taft on the first ballot. Overall, Ike was nine votes short of the nomination. Fine jumped up and tried to get recognized to switch the Taft votes to Ike before the vote was recorded, but the convention chairman would not recognize him. Minnesota delivered the majority, much to the dismay of a stunned Fine and the

Supporters of 1952 Democratic nominee Adlai Stevenson anxiously record election night returns at his Philadelphia campaign headquarters. Despite great success in Philadelphia and a general trend towards Democratic control of the city, Stevenson lost the election to Republican Dwight Eisenhower. (Temple University Libraries, Urban Archives)

Pennsylvania delegation. He was criticized in the national media for his behavior. Fine never recovered from the national humiliation.[28]

During the fall campaign, the Democrats were on the defensive. The Republican themes were Korea, corruption, and communism. Stevenson had to defend the Truman administration's policies. Richard M. Nixon, the Republican vice presidential candidate, attacked Stevenson directly by calling him "Adlai, the Appeaser," a reference to the charge that the Illinois governor would be soft on communism if elected. Not allowing his record to go undefended, Truman took to the stump, traveling 18,000 miles, challenging Ike's plans for ending the war. Eisenhower mostly took the high road, appearing genial and exuding personal warmth. He also was reassuring on the stalemate in the war, especially within ten days of the election when he promised to go to Korea. Since the 1952 election was primarily about the war and foreign affairs, the war hero's experience in these matters proved decisive.

The Republicans swept the country, winning the presidency for the first time since 1928. Eisenhower won 55 percent of the popular vote and 442 electoral votes to Stevenson's 44 percent and only 89 electoral votes. Stevenson managed to win only nine states, and most of them in the South.

In Pennsylvania, the Eisenhower victory was narrow, but the Republicans were gleeful. Ike won 53 percent of the popular vote and carried fifty-eight counties, leaving the Democrats with Philadelphia in the southeast, Lackawanna in the northeast, and seven southwestern counties. Still, Stevenson managed 47 percent of the vote.

The 1952 presidential election augured a new potential for competitiveness in Pennsylvania politics. The popular Eisenhower reduced Stevenson's big-city vote advantage in Pittsburgh, losing in Allegheny County by a mere 12,000 votes, and Stevenson won the Democratic southwestern counties by reduced margins. The bright moment for the Democrats came in Philadelphia. Stevenson won there by 160,000 votes; Truman had carried the Quaker City by a mere 7,000 in 1948. Stevenson's victory was accomplished by running up wide margins in virtually every working-class white and black neighborhood and by lesser margins in the more affluent sections of the city. The Stevenson campaign benefited from the atrophy of the Republican City Committee, the development of a genuine Democratic organization, and a substantial Stevenson volunteer organization of independents and liberal activists. The big vote for Stevenson, when combined with the victories of reform Democrats Joe Clark and Richardson Dilworth in the 1951 city contests, solidified the transition of Philadelphia from a Republican to a Democratic city. It paved the way for a competitive two-party state to emerge, while inaugurating an era of one-party Democratic rule in the state's largest city.

1956: Eisenhower and Stevenson

The 1956 presidential election was a reprise of 1952. Although Eisenhower was personally very popular during his time in the White House, the Democrats stormed back in the 1954 midterm elections to pick up fourteen seats in the Senate and fifty-two seats in the House. During Ike's first term he had supported the expansion of a variety of federal programs, including Social Security, the minimum wage, and funding for low-income housing. In his reelection year, he also advocated and accomplished the largest expansion of the federal highway system in history. Only a serious heart attack in 1955 made his reelection problematic, but as the Republican convention drew near in August, it was apparent that Ike's health had improved sufficiently for him to run. After a brief flurry of activity surrounding the question of whether Richard Nixon should be renominated for vice president, the San Francisco Republican national convention unanimously approved the Eisenhower-Nixon ticket for the second time.

As the campaign season opened, Pennsylvania Democratic leaders solidly backed Adlai Stevenson to repeat as his party's nominee. His supporters included Governor George M. Leader; former Philadelphia mayor Joe Clark, the eventual Democratic nominee for the U.S. Senate in 1956; and most other Democratic leaders in the state. By 1952, Clark had become a devoted advocate for Stevenson, even helping the Illinois governor write a speech dealing with urban problems and solutions for the annual Conference of the American Municipal Association. The one exception among the state's top Democratic leaders was Congressman William J. Green Jr. of Philadelphia, a possible U.S. Senate candidate, who had a close relationship with Stevenson's main rival, Senator Kefauver. When Green decided not to contest Clark for the Senate nomination, his statewide influence waned, and virtually the entire Pennsylvania delegation went to Chicago committed to Stevenson.

Stevenson's national campaign was directed by a Pennsylvania Democratic leader, James A. Finnegan, who resigned his position as Secretary of the Commonwealth to run the Stevenson campaign. Finnegan was deeply tied to Philadelphia politics. A former member of the Philadelphia Democratic Party leadership and a city council member, he also was a political confidante of Joe Clark. In June 1956, Finnegan sent Clark an optimistic assessment of the Democratic nomination contest. He essentially made three arguments: first, that Stevenson had overwhelmingly won the Pennsylvania primary even when faced with a write-in campaign by his opponents; second, that the Illinois governor had traveled all over the country in 1954 campaigning for Democrats in their successful mid-term congressional efforts; and third, in contrast to his reluctance in 1952, Stevenson had just traveled more than 65,000 miles to earn the nomination. Moreover, Finnegan continued, Stevenson was forthright and vigorous in going after the Eisenhower administration for allowing foreign policy abroad to drift and for a lack of a domestic agenda.[29]

The Democrats had a brief but intense early primary battle between Estes Kefauver and Adlai Stevenson. Beyond that, it was largely a Stevenson romp. He had about two-thirds of the votes necessary for the nomination by the time the Chicago convention opened for business, though several names were put in nomination at the convention. His first-ballot victory was capped by Pennsylvania's new governor, George Leader, who threw the state's 67 votes to Stevenson, giving him the majority for nomination and triggering a raucous demonstration.

Stevenson then shocked the convention by not recommending a running mate, throwing the choice over to party leaders. Several possibilities quickly emerged: Senator Albert A. Gore Sr. of Tennessee (father of the future vice president and presidential candidate); one future president, Senator John F. Kennedy of Massachusetts; and another future vice president and presidential candidate, Senator Hubert H. Humphrey of Minnesota. The contest settled into a battle between Kennedy and Kefauver, and Kefauver eventually won.[30]

The fall election was a mismatch. Ike was one of the few two-term presidents who wore well with the voters. The Stevenson campaign, fighting vigorously but out-gunned, made the most of a series of arguments for a "New America." Republicans boasted, "Everything is booming but the guns," an obvious reference to prosperity and no war. Yet prospects for war loomed. Several weeks before the 1956 election, the Soviet Union invaded Hungary and on November 1, the French and the British seized the Suez Canal, which created an unstable situation in the volatile Middle East. These events made Stevenson's task more difficult because of voters' reluctance to change parties when facing controversial international situations.

Pennsylvania's Democratic leaders were not very optimistic either as they prepared for the fall campaign. A statewide Democratic poll conducted by Lou Harris in August found Stevenson about where he stood in 1952, but figures for Philadelphia and Pittsburgh showed that the Illinois governor had slipped in support. The poll found enhanced strength in other regions of the state. But unfortunately for the Democrats, Harris found that the voters in rural and small cites were less interested in the election and more generally apathetic about the issues of the campaign.

The Pennsylvania election returns bore out the Harris poll's findings. Eisenhower won 56 percent to Stevenson's 43 percent, and the president captured an amazing sixty-two counties, reducing the Democrats to Philadelphia and four southwestern counties, Fayette, Greene, Westmoreland, and Washington. Stevenson lost several Democratic strongholds: Allegheny County by 69,000, Lackawanna by 9,000, Beaver by 1,900, and Cambria by 4,600. The Democrats had not lost Allegheny, Beaver, and Cambria since 1928, and Lackawanna since 1924. Philadelphia's former mayor, Joe Clark, swam alone against the Republican tide. Despite Ike's 600,000-vote victory, Clark defeated Senator Jim Duff's reelection bid by a narrow 20,000-vote margin. The Republicans regained control of the state House and retained control of the state Senate. They also won both statewide row offices and a majority of the congressional delegation from the state.

Nationally, Ike captured 57 percent of the popular vote with Stevenson winning 42 percent. The electoral vote count was even more disastrous for the Democrats; Ike won 86 percent or 457 votes to Stevenson's 14 percent and only 73 electoral votes. Stevenson won only seven states, and none in the Northeast, the upper Midwest, or the West.

The Eisenhower victories in the state in the 1950s were, in the long run, not devastating for the Democrats. They won back-to-back governorships in 1954 and 1958, one of the three U.S. Senate elections, and two of three races for the office of secretary of internal affairs. Though they lost the elections for state treasurer and auditor general, the long-term statewide prospect for the Democrats had improved markedly. The 1950s were a transitional decade that completed the political dynamics begun during the New Deal years. The state became competitive in statewide races, not just in the short run but for the next fifty years. Pennsylvania, once the forgotten state in presidential general elections, would move center stage nationally, commanding the attention of presidential candidates and the national media.

After a speech at the Academy of Music, President Dwight Eisenhower waves to a Philadelphia crowd while campaigning for his vice president and 1960 Republican nominee Richard Nixon. As the politician most associated with the 1950s, Eisenhower achieved electoral success in Pennsylvania that Republicans hoped to match in the next decade. (Temple University Libraries, Urban Archives)

Chapter 4
The Competitive State: the 1960s

By 1960, Pennsylvania had become a competitive state. The Democrats, who began the 1950s with less than 40 percent of registered voters, secured a slight edge in registration for the first time in history when they reached 51 percent by 1960. They led Republicans by 2,965 voters out of 5.6 million registrants in the two parties. Through the 1960s the voter registration margin remained remarkably close. By the 1968 election the Republicans narrowly reversed the margin, gaining a 50 percent to 49 percent edge over the Democrats. The state had gone from being one of the least competitive of the northern states to one of the most competitive, and the decade of the 1960s would illustrate just how competitive the state had become.

Intense two-party competition also generated increased turnout. Voter turnout in presidential elections in the 1960s reached its highest point since the second decade of the twentieth century (and the exceptionally high turnout of 1936), with a 71 percent turnout in 1960, 68 percent in 1964, and 67 percent in 1968.[31]

Tough competition extended to presidential elections. John F. Kennedy carried the state by less than two percentage points to begin the decade, and, though Lyndon Johnson won the state in a landslide in 1964, the last presidential election of the decade was competitive. The winning candidate, Richard M. Nixon, won by four percentage points. In the 1960s the state had one Republican and one Democratic U.S. senator for almost the entire decade. The governorship began to change party hands with clock-like precision every eight years. The legislature became very volatile, especially the state House, which was likely to change with the party that carried the governorship or the presidency in the state. Truly, a two-party state had become a reality.

1960: Kennedy and Nixon

As the 1960 presidential election approached, the big political question facing the country was whether the Republicans could hold onto the White House without the popular Eisenhower at the head of the ticket. And the Republicans had much to worry about. At home unemployment exceeded 6 percent, and abroad the U-2 incident, in which the Soviets shot down an American surveillance plane, unsettled the nation, and the launching of the first Soviet satellite into space pushed the Cold War into a new phase.

The Republican nomination was a forgone conclusion. Waiting dutifully in the wings was Vice President Richard Nixon. The vice president had worked closely with party leaders during his time in office, especially campaigning on behalf of the party's local, state, and congressional candidates. Virtually the entire Republican establishment was behind him, including the financial contributors. One exception was outgoing President Eisenhower, who remained aloof from the campaign until its final days. But Ike's failure to help his vice president did not hinder Nixon's run at the nomination. For example, Nixon won the Pennsylvania April primary; he earned almost one million popular votes to 10,000 write-in ballots for the new governor of New York, Nelson A. Rockefeller, who at the time was not an announced candidate.[32]

As the Democrats convened in Los Angeles, their nomination was a more complicated affair. Reluctant to nominate Stevenson after his two defeats by Eisenhower, the Los Angeles convention turned to Senator John F. Kennedy, who succeeded in his four-year effort to become the nominee but not before a difficult struggle. Kennedy had been in the U.S. Senate since 1953, and he almost won the vice presidential nomination in 1956. Though he did not have a particularly distinguished Senate career, he was ambitious and charismatic. For many years his

John F. Kennedy addresses a crowd in Lancaster's Penn Square during his campaign for the presidency in 1960. The 1960 presidential election marked Pennsylvania as a highly competitive, two-party battleground state, culminating a trend that began with the election of Franklin D. Roosevelt in 1932. (Lancaster *New Era*)

wealthy father, Joseph P. Kennedy Sr., a former ambassador to Great Britain, had been preparing the way for a national presidential campaign for his son.

Kennedy's nomination was no sure thing. The 1960 campaign year often has been referred to as the year of the senatorial candidates. The Kennedy forces had to deal with several strong U.S. Senate opponents: Lyndon B. Johnson of Texas, Hubert H. Humphrey of Minnesota, W. Stuart Symington of Missouri, and several favorite sons. The redoubtable Adlai Stevenson also waited in the wings for any opening. The primary contests were fought out between Kennedy and Humphrey, with Kennedy scoring victories in ethnically and industrially diverse Wisconsin and in heavily Protestant West Virginia – the latter a test of the Catholic Kennedy's ability to win Protestant voters. In Pennsylvania, Kennedy also won easily. Johnson's hopes were pinned on southern delegates, and Symington hung back waiting for the convention to convene, hoping that a deadlocked convention might turn to him. As the Democrats assembled in Los Angeles in early July, the nominee was not yet decided, but the Kennedy momentum was strong.[33]

If opponents wanted to stop Kennedy, they would need to keep the various favorite-son candidates from getting out of the race and throwing votes to Kennedy. Interestingly, two years earlier Kennedy thought his main rival for the Democratic nomination would be the popular mayor of Philadelphia, Richardson Dilworth. Elected mayor in 1955 as part of the reform movement that crushed the Republican political machine in the city, Dilworth was considered briefly a rising national star in the Democratic Party. However, his inability to win statewide office severely diminished any national prospects. His best prospect was the governorship in 1958, the year the Democrats won with Pittsburgh mayor and party boss David Lawrence. Dilworth passed on a candidacy that year, and the decision was viewed as a critical mistake for any future presidential ambitions.

At the Los Angeles convention, the key player in the Pennsylvania delegation was in fact Governor David Lawrence, the political boss who already was a veteran of party convention politics. He had become chairman of the State Democratic Party in 1936, then worked diligently and shrewdly to ensure an FDR sweep of the state. He was one of the few politicians who successfully made the transition from political boss to respected office holder. As Pittsburgh's mayor and as governor, he pursued the progressive policies of FDR's New Deal and Truman's Fair Deal. As much as anyone, he had control over the Pennsylvania Democratic Party and most of the delegates in Los Angeles. He commanded deep respect within the state delegation, but at the outset of the presidential campaign he was a man in personal conflict. One reason for the conflict was his adulation of Adlai Stevenson, which bordered on hero worship. Even though Stevenson's nomination was the long shot of long shots, Lawrence was reluctant to move the delegation to support Kennedy. In addition, he had real concerns that a Catholic could not win the presidency. A Catholic himself, he and some other Catholic political leaders were convinced that after the virulent anti-Catholic reaction to the presidential campaign of Al Smith in 1928, Kennedy would run afoul of the same prejudice. Lawrence also recognized that his Catholicism had cost him votes among some Protestants in his gubernatorial victory in 1958, though many voters were probably unaware of Lawrence's religious affiliation. Kennedy's father realized Lawrence's importance and asked another party leader, Matt McCloskey, to visit the governor to encourage an endorsement for his son. McCloskey's entreaty was unsuccessful; Lawrence wanted to wait until a consensus for a candidate emerged. When McCloskey reported the failed effort, Joseph Kennedy reacted angrily and went to Harrisburg himself, but his attempt also proved futile.

Soon it became evident that Lawrence's goal of keeping the Pennsylvania delegation neutral was coming apart. Kennedy was developing considerable support among the Democratic rank and file in the state, as evidenced by a huge write-in vote for him in the spring primary; he garnered more than 183,000 votes to 27,000 for Stevenson. Lawrence also had to consider the endorsements of Kennedy by other Democratic leaders, including Senator Joseph Clark, Philadelphia powerhouse Congressman William Green, future Governor Milton J. Shapp, and a bevy of county leaders.

As the national convention opened, the Pennsylvania delegation remained divided but leaned heavily to Kennedy. The three active candidates, Kennedy, Symington, and Johnson, made their pitches to the delegation, and Kennedy received a rousing standing ovation when he appeared. The first inside-the-caucus test vote gave Kennedy 64 of the 81 votes. Lawrence reluctantly gave Kennedy his support after it was apparent a deadlocked convention was not going to occur, and Stevenson had no chance to be the nominee. The state delegation put up 68 Kennedy votes in the first and only presidential nomination roll call. Kennedy swept to an easy 806 to 409 vote victory over Johnson. Lawrence made one of the seconding speeches for the Massachusetts senator.

Lawrence's work was not finished. Kennedy chose Lyndon Johnson as his running mate, but not before a measure of politics and intrigue. This decision was momentous, fraught with important consequences for the general election. Lawrence was among a group of national party leaders who urged Kennedy to make Johnson his running mate in order to shore up southern votes. Lawrence's biographer, Michael Weber, relates the story that the press of people milling around Kennedy's hotel suite after his nomination vote forced Kennedy, Lawrence, and Matt McCloskey into the senator's bathroom for their private conversation about the vice presidential nomination. Kennedy wanted to be sure that Johnson would accept the nomination if offered, and Lawrence assured him he would accept. Lawrence and other party leaders had Johnson's prior assurance to indicate he would accept. Shortly thereafter, Kennedy made the offer, against the wishes of organized labor and his own brother, Robert.[34]

Candidate debates had been part of political life since colonial times, but the practice had not extended to presidential contests. In 1960 Kennedy challenged Nixon to a series of debates, four in all. Most historians agree that Kennedy's performance, especially in the first debate, made a fundamental difference in the election outcome. Nixon's performance was mediocre; he looked fatigued, and he perspired profusely. He did, as expected, have a command of the debate subject matter, given his considerable experience as a member of Congress and vice president for almost eight years, but Kennedy's performance was better and strong enough to convince many voters that despite his relative youthfulness and inexperience, he was ready to be president. The Gallup poll taken immediately after the first debate on September 26 showed Kennedy with a lead for the first time in the campaign.

Kennedy's Catholicism, as Governor Lawrence feared, turned out to be one of the most important concerns the candidate needed to overcome. An earlier 1959 Gallup poll provided concrete evidence that religion would be an important hurdle. One in four voters told Gallup that they would not vote for a qualified Catholic candidate. Many in the southern wing of JFK's own party feared the election of a Catholic. A Catholic had not been elected president before, and the concern was that he would not be free to exercise independent judgment on state matters if they differed from church teaching or be free from papal direction. Kennedy, in what proved to be a brilliant tactical move, addressed a group of hostile Protestant ministers in September in Houston, where he pledged to keep church and state matters separate – a principle he called absolute. This effort to defuse the issue has been seen as a defining moment of the campaign, but it did not stop the rampant anti-Catholicism in parts of the country.

And it was not just a southern party problem. In Pennsylvania, accounts of rising anti-Catholicism and religious bigotry were widespread, leading to increased voter registration and larger turnout in parts of the state with more conservative religious denominations. No one captured this sentiment more clearly than one of the nation's most distinguished fiction writers, James Michener, who served as a surrogate for Kennedy nationally and as head of the Kennedy campaign in Bucks County. After the election he wrote a detailed account of his political activities in a little-read but informative book called *Report of the County Chairman*. He described the rising religious bigotry in Bucks County generated because of the Kennedy candidacy. Michener saw anti-Catholicism as more widespread than just among the German Lutherans and Mennonites who lived in the northern and central parts of the county. Michener described some aspects of the bigotry, from pamphlets depicting Catholic prelates torturing Protestants to hate literature mailed anonymously to homes. He believed these activities were part of an organized campaign, and he concluded that the religious issue permeated every aspect of the 1960 contest. The author later unsuccessfully sought a congressional seat in Bucks County, and in 1972 he toured the state as a speaker for the presidential effort of Senator Edmund S. Muskie of Maine.[35]

Kennedy and Nixon campaigned heavily in the state. The Massachusetts senator developed what became known as the "big state" strategy. He would spend the final three weeks of the campaign stumping through the large electoral vote states of the Northeast, where he was greeted by huge and enthusiastic crowds. Typical of the rhetoric he used in campaign events in the latter days of the campaign were the arguments he made in a public appearance in Levittown, Bucks County, on October 30 as the campaign rolled to a conclusion. The senator told a responsive crowd that the country needed new leadership, a theme he had repeatedly emphasized during the campaign. He also criticized the Republicans for their failure to support programs enacted over the previous twenty-five years, such as housing, Social Security, and minimum wage. He focused most of his attention on future employment, suggesting that the Republicans would not provide the 25,000 jobs the economy would need for the next eight years.

Vice President and 1960 Republican nominee Richard Nixon strikes an iconic pose while greeting a crowd of supporters at Philadelphia's Convention Hall. (Temple University Libraries, Urban Archives)

Despite Nixon's decision to honor his pledge to campaign in all fifty states, he managed several campaign swings through Pennsylvania in middle and late October. He stressed his usual themes that Kennedy was too inexperienced to be president, and that he was far too critical of the United States; Nixon called it "running America down." He also stressed that Kennedy's government programs would hurt the average working person by causing inflation. By the campaign's end, Nixon was also a candidate in search of empathy from the voters, appealing to their hearts as much as to their minds. During one Pennsylvania visit he talked about the death of his 77-year-old father, who left a large medical bill unpaid. Nixon insisted he was not opposed to helping those in need and that he understood the concerns of his fellow countrymen. In the eastern part of the state, he made an unscheduled stop at the home of the aging Delaware County Republican Party boss, John McClure, largely to help offset the expected strong showing among the large Catholic population in that blue-collar county. At the end of a close, hard-fought, and bitter campaign, President Eisenhower and former President Truman both appeared in Pittsburgh on the same day to deliver campaign speeches for their parties' candidates.[36]

Catholic voters were pivotal in 1960 and were more sought out politically than in any election in American history. Importantly, their numbers had swelled to 40 million and as a whole they had become more upwardly mobile since the New Deal years. Nationally, the Democratic vote among Catholics had declined in 1952 and in 1956. Kennedy's Catholicism reversed that slide. It is now generally recognized that Kennedy's Catholicism proved decisive in his victory. The Catholic vote increased by 2 million over 1956, while the turnout of Protestants went up about 4.5 million. What mattered most was that Kennedy's Catholic vote was more concentrated in big industrial electoral vote states with substantial Catholic populations, providing the electoral vote difference for him in those key states. Motivating Catholics to vote was part of the Kennedy big industrial state strategy in Pennsylvania, Illinois, Ohio, New Jersey, and New York. Eisenhower had won the five in 1952 and 1956, but JFK won four of the five in 1960, losing only Ohio.

In Pennsylvania, Catholics comprised about 30 percent of the state's adult population. The increased support for Kennedy in the counties with large numbers of Catholics was remarkable. Allegheny, Westmoreland, Beaver, Cambria, Erie, Philadelphia, and Lackawanna had large Catholic populations, ranging from 26 percent in Beaver to 38 percent in Cambria and Westmoreland, and all of them had large increases in voter turnout. JFK's 330,000-vote edge in Philadelphia, three times Stevenson's 1956 margin, was impressive and in part resulted from the prodigious work of Democratic Party head Bill Green. Conversely, Nixon ran well in the heavily Protestant counties located in the south-central part of the state, where Anabaptists (Amish and Mennonites), especially in Lancaster County, registered and voted in some cases for the first time.[37]

A Philadelphia husband and wife express their contrary preference towards the 1960 presidential candidates while their daughter attempts to stay above the fray. In 1960, both John F. Kennedy and Richard Nixon campaigned heavily across Pennsylvania with Kennedy's narrow victory in the state reflecting the close national margin between the two candidates. (Temple University Libraries, Urban Archives)

Overall, Kennedy's victory in Pennsylvania was narrow, 51 percent to 49 percent, or 116,000 out of five million votes cast. He won fifteen counties. Kennedy's national vote mirrored the Pennsylvania vote. He defeated Nixon 49.7 percent to 49.6 percent, or about one vote per precinct, the closest election since 1880. The electoral vote was more decisive, 303 votes to 219. JFK's running mate, Lyndon Johnson, helped the ticket hold onto most of the Deep South – without which Nixon would have won the presidency.[38]

1964: Johnson and Goldwater

The assassination of President Kennedy in November 1963 left the nation in a state of emotional recovery as Vice President Johnson took the reins of the presidency. Leaving no doubt he was in charge, Johnson immediately launched a series of bold legislative initiatives that changed the nature of the federal government and American society. He moved on several fronts: a tax cut, civil rights, and an initiative he called the "War on Poverty." He succeeded on all three fronts during 1964 – the tax cut in February, the momentous Civil Rights Act in July, and the Economic Opportunity Act in August. With Johnson's impressive legislative accomplishments, he had little trouble winning his party's nomination. He passed over the slain president's brother, Robert F. Kennedy, for his vice presidential selection, and chose instead liberal icon Senator Hubert H. Humphrey of Minnesota, one of the major architects of the civil rights law just passed by Congress.

As LBJ took the country to the left, the Republicans moved sharply to the right. They nominated Senator Barry M. Goldwater of Arizona. Goldwater had a narrow view of the role of the federal government. He wanted smaller government and a tougher stance on communism. His conservative wing of the party had chafed for decades as the Republicans nominated a string of moderates for president, and finally in 1964 the conservatives prevailed. Goldwater might be best described, however, as a libertarian, especially given his opposition to the expansion of the federal government: he opposed the progressive income tax, federal support for education, welfare, and farm subsidies. But it was his answer to a Social Security question during the January New Hampshire primary that received considerable press coverage and would haunt his political career, and not just in 1964. He suggested that the best system would be a voluntary one – translation, Goldwater would end Social Security. He did favor expanding the nation's defense program, and he bitterly opposed any accommodationist policies with the Soviet Union.

The moderate wing of the party did not acquiesce to the inevitability of Goldwater's nomination. The logical choice was Richard Nixon, who had lost by a whisker in 1960. But after his humiliating defeat in the 1962 California gubernatorial race, Nixon refused to run, even though he led the field of Republican potential candidates in a spring 1964 Gallup poll. As other moderates failed to stop

An enthusiastic crowd at the Philadelphia International Airport greets President Lyndon Johnson during a campaign visit in 1964. In this election, Johnson's margin of victory in Allegheny County and Philadelphia were substantial and marked new heights in Democratic dominance of these areas of the state. (Temple University Libraries, Urban Archives)

the Goldwater juggernaut, their last best hope was the late entry into the race by William W. Scranton, the recently elected governor of Pennsylvania. Scranton had won election by almost half a million votes in 1962. Speculation ensued almost immediately among journalists and Republican insiders that the newly elected big-state governor might be a future presidential candidate.

A millionaire whose ancestors founded the city of Scranton, the new governor had been the hand-picked gubernatorial candidate of a small group of state Republican powerbrokers desperate to avoid an internecine primary war between Superior Court Judge Robert E. Woodside from Millersburg in Dauphin County and Senator Hugh Scott. Scranton had served only a single term in the U.S. House of Representatives, elected in 1961 from the Scranton-based Democratic district that John Kennedy carried easily in 1960. Following his election to Congress, he was mentioned as a potential national Republican candidate. Although a Republican, Scranton had personal ties to the Kennedy family. He and

President Kennedy had been friends in college, and Scranton had dated Kennedy's sister Kathleen. In Congress, he often supported Kennedy's congressional agenda. Taking office as governor in 1963, Scranton quickly gained the state legislature's support for a tax package to end the state's fiscal crisis. He proceeded to obtain the passage of progressive legislation: tough strip mine controls, liberalized medical care for seniors, expanded civil service coverage, modernized professional licensing procedures, and increased spending on a variety of state programs, notably education.[39]

During the winter and the early spring primary season, Scranton remained neutral, avoiding any overt sign of support for a candidate or pursuing a candidacy of his own. He did indicate in a January 9, 1964, press conference in Washington that he was not a favorite-son candidate, but he might become one if state Republicans asked him and if the nomination contest did not become a rout in favor of one of the candidates. As time passed, the governor came under enormous pressure to run, especially as the other anti-Goldwater candidates, George W. Romney and Nelson A. Rockefeller, were eliminated from the contest. Finally Scranton called a press conference on April 9 and announced that while he was not a candidate, he would permit his name to be used as a favorite son. Scranton's own top staffers, despite orders to the contrary, organized a write-in campaign for the April 28 Pennsylvania primary. They set a target of 300,000 votes and came close to the mark. Scranton won 220,000, or about 58 percent, to Henry Cabot Lodge's 21 percent, Richard Nixon's 10 percent, and Nelson Rockefeller's 2 percent.[40]

Scranton ended the suspense in a June 13 speech to the Maryland State Republican Convention in Baltimore when he announced that he would seek the Republican nomination. Several factors finally pushed Scranton to declare. He had been hearing from fellow Republican office holders that a Goldwater candidacy would lead scores of them to defeat. Personally, he was appalled at Goldwater's hostility to the federal government's poverty programs, but the final straw was the vote Goldwater cast in the Senate to invoke cloture when the civil rights bill came to the Senate floor – in effect, a vote against the bill. There was one other important consideration. On June 2, five days after Goldwater won the California primary, President Eisenhower invited Scranton to his Gettysburg home for a meeting. The Pennsylvania governor left the meeting with the distinct impression that the former president wanted him to run and that the party would benefit from an open convention. But several days later, Eisenhower told Scranton by phone that the cause was hopeless because Goldwater's nomination could not be stopped, and he did not want to see the party rent by further dissention over the nomination.[41] Eisenhower was correct; the Scranton candidacy was hopeless from the start. Of the 1,300 total delegates, Goldwater had almost 600 committed to him at the time of Scranton's announcement. Not to be denied, however, the

A late entrant into the race for the 1964 Republican nomination, Pennsylvania Governor William W. Scranton waves to the crowd at a campaign stop in Minneapolis. Here, the lone sign in support of Barry Goldwater proved prescient, as Scranton subsequently lost the nomination to Goldwater at the party's convention in San Francisco. (Temple University Libraries, Urban Archives)

Pennsylvania governor embarked on a twenty-five-state, thirty-two-day, million-dollar effort to drum up support. He also met with various state convention delegations in an attempt to stop the Arizona senator. He was spectacularly unsuccessful, but in three public polls conducted on the eve of the San Francisco convention, Scranton was the overwhelming favorite of the Republican voters in the nation.

Scranton could do nothing to stop Goldwater's inexorable drive to the nomination, and not even a national appeal for voters to write and telegram their support for Scranton made a difference, although half a million responded. The Pennsylvania delegates were resigned to defeat, but not dispirited when they arrived in early July in San Francisco. Scranton's floor manager, Senator Scott, worked tirelessly against insuperable odds. Following precedent, Scranton did not attend the convention sessions, but he kept up a heavy schedule visiting with state delegations. All the while, he publicly denied that he had any interest in the vice presidential nomination or that former President Eisenhower had attempted to persuade him to take the second spot.

Eisenhower may not have encouraged Scranton to join the Republican ticket, but three years later when assessing the Republican field for the 1968 presidential election, Ike was not reticent at all in suggesting to journalist Roscoe Drummond that Scranton was his first choice for the Republican nomination. When Scranton left the governorship in January 1967, he pledged that he would not seek elective office again. Ike tried on numerous occasions to convince the governor to renounce his pledge, but Scranton held firm, despite assurances from Eisenhower that he would campaign openly and forcefully for him.

The Pennsylvania governor struggled mightily against overwhelming odds as the nomination vote approached, and he seemingly became more desperate as his cause became more hopeless. He had barely criticized Goldwater at the outset of his candidacy, but by the eve of the convention he was attacking Goldwater for his civil rights vote, his belief that the Tennessee Valley Authority should be sold, and especially his idea that military commanders should have the authority to use tactical nuclear weapons.

On Wednesday, July 15, Milton Eisenhower, the former president's brother, put Scranton's name in nomination. But it took only thirty minutes on the first ballot for Goldwater to end Scranton's presidential dreams: the count was decisive, 883 to 214. One small consolation for Scranton was the support of his own state delegation, the third-largest at the convention. The delegates gave him 60 of their 64 votes. After his loss, Scranton assured the convention he would support and campaign for Goldwater. He did campaign despite deeply held fears that Goldwater's candidacy would cause irreparable harm to other Republican candidates in the state and country.

Strange as it might seem – because of the nomination competition and the ideological differences – Scranton and Goldwater had been good friends earlier in their careers. When Scranton had worked in Washington in 1959 as an assistant to Secretary of State Christian A. Herter, Goldwater was Scranton's superior officer in a Capitol Hill Air Force reserve unit. The two had grown friendly and corresponded frequently: they even shipped out together on NATO exercises in 1959. Goldwater later claimed Scranton was his first choice for a running mate before the Pennsylvania governor entered the nomination fray. But the bitterness of the nomination struggle personally aggrieved Goldwater and ended any possibility of a Scranton addition to the ticket. A Scranton choice was not to be, but it would have provided ideological balance and broadened the appeal of the ticket.[42]

Goldwater did not try to unify the party after his nomination. He chose another staunch conservative for a running mate, Congressman William E. Miller of New York. He then made one of the most ideological speeches in convention history, finishing it off with his campaign's clarion call: "Extremism in the defense of liberty is no vice. Moderation in pursuit of justice is no virtue." The Goldwater strategy for victory lay in the old Confederacy, the Rocky Mountain states, and a few Republican midwestern states. Pennsylvania was left out of the political calculus. The Goldwater campaign wrote off the state. During the final week of the campaign, the Arizonan did whistle-stop through the state, mostly trying to defend himself against the charge that he would end Social Security if elected. But little more was done to win the Keystone State.

Many Republican moderates continued to believe that the party was in deep trouble in the fall election. Pennsylvania Senator Hugh Scott was particularly pessimistic about the prospect of losing legislative and congressional seats, but he endorsed the ticket even though it imperiled his own reelection to the Senate. Amazingly, in an incredible display of ticket-splitting, Scott won reelection by 71,000 votes while Lyndon Johnson carried the state by almost 1.5 million votes.

The election outcome was never in doubt. Incumbents serving during times of peace and a healthy economy are always difficult if not impossible to defeat. And Goldwater was far too conservative for the nation's voters. Johnson spent the early fall ensconced in the White House, governing and remaining above the campaign fray. He finally hit the trail in October and was greeted by huge and enthusiastic crowds. Goldwater presented an easy target. The senator ran as a candidate committed to a series of causes, but he never articulated an alternative vision to Johnson's pragmatic campaign. The president campaigned on the promise to extend the social safety net, expand voting rights, and create jobs – all part of the post-election Great Society. Johnson's campaign could easily target Goldwater as the enemy of the modern welfare state, especially with his opposition to Social Security. The Democrats also raised the specter that Goldwater could not be trusted to govern in the nuclear age. The now famous "daisy commercial," showing a young girl standing in a field counting daisy petals when the screen blackens and a nuclear mushroom cloud appears, aired only once, on September 7, 1964, but it left a lasting impression that Goldwater would lead the nation into a nuclear war.

Johnson's 61 percent national victory matched the percentage won by FDR in 1936. Johnson won 486 electoral votes to Goldwater's 52, or 90 percent of the total available. The Arizona senator managed to win only six states, all southern with the exception of Goldwater's home state, Arizona. Culminating the landslide, the Democrats picked up seats in the Senate and House and now had comfortable majorities in both: 68 to 32 in the Senate and 295 to 140 in the House.

Scranton and Scott proved prescient in their concern that Goldwater's candidacy would lead to electoral disaster for state Republicans. The Republicans were massacred: they lost two statewide offices, the auditor general and state treasurer, two statewide judgeships, two congressional seats, and control of the state House. In Pennsylvania, LBJ won a spectacular 65 percent of the vote to Goldwater's 35 percent; the state's 29 electoral votes for Johnson were never in doubt. Roosevelt had won forty-one counties for the Democrats in 1936; Johnson surpassed that with a sixty-three county victory. Goldwater only won Union, Lebanon, Wayne, and Snyder counties. He even lost Lancaster County, though by fewer than 1,000 votes; Lancaster had not gone Democratic since before the Civil War. Chester County fell to the Democrats for the first time since 1912, when Woodrow Wilson eked out a narrow 35 percent victory over Theodore Roosevelt, who managed 33 percent, and William Howard Taft, who ran a close third with 29 percent. The Allegheny and Philadelphia majorities for the president were majestic in their magnitude, 234,000 and 431,000, respectively.[43]

The 1964 presidential election defied normal voting patterns in the state. The one-sidedness of the outcome was largely a product of the special circumstances that surrounded the election, namely the success of Johnson's legislative program and the ultra-conservatism of Barry Goldwater.

1968: Nixon and Humphrey

Numerous problems plagued the Johnson administration by 1968; by far the most important one was the growing unpopularity of the Vietnam War. The first event that affected the 1968 presidential election was the seizure of the USS Pueblo by communist North Korea. The second and more damaging occurred only a week later when the Viet Cong and the North Vietnamese Army launched the Tet offensive, a coordinated assault on major American installations throughout South Vietnam, notably on the U.S. embassy in Saigon. The attack ultimately failed, but it gave the appearance that the enemy was not being defeated, and for the first time public polls reflected the attitude that the war should end.

A growing anti-war movement fueled the candidacy of Minnesota Senator Eugene J. McCarthy, who used Tet to gain momentum. Then the first of several political shock waves of the new year occurred. In early March, Johnson won the New Hampshire primary, but McCarthy received an impressive 42 percent of the vote. Senator Robert F. Kennedy of New York, the brother of President Kennedy and a passionate critic of the war, sensed an opening and declared his candidacy a few days after the primary. He became the second major candidate to oppose the war. Then, stunningly, Johnson announced at the end of the month that he was dropping out of the presidential race. After that, in early

Volunteers speak with North Philadelphia residents during a non-partisan voter registration drive in 1968. (Temple University Libraries, Urban Archives)

April, civil rights leader Martin Luther King Jr. was assassinated and riots broke out in cities across the country. Another shock wave followed the assassination of Robert Kennedy on the evening of his victory in the June California primary. As traumatic as the events of the first six months of 1968 were, more would follow.

With the president on the sidelines, Vice President Hubert H. Humphrey joined the list of candidates on April 27. His strategy was not to wage battle in the primaries and caucuses but to line up support among Democratic political regulars and power brokers – the big-city party bosses, union leaders, and state leaders. Humphrey was renowned as a champion of civil rights and liberal social legislation, but he was a staunch supporter of the war.

In Pennsylvania, which held its primary four days before Humphrey's announcement, Eugene McCarthy was the only candidate to enter formally the presidential primary of either party. Other candidates waged write-in campaigns. McCarthy won slightly more than 400,000 votes, 77 percent of the total. Robert Kennedy led the write-ins with 61,000 to Humphrey's 41,000. Even though he was not a candidate, Johnson received 16,000 die-hard loyalist votes.

What might seem at first glance to be a popular state sweep for McCarthy did not translate into a delegate victory. Pennsylvania Democrats had 130 convention delegates going to the national convention, but two factors were relevant to the disposition of the delegates. First, the primary vote was not binding on the delegates. Delegates elected at the local level for the most part ran unpledged, meaning that, as historically had been the case, they were free to vote for whomever they pleased at the convention. Party regulars determined to vote for Humphrey successfully ran as delegate candidates throughout the state, although they were officially listed as uncommitted. The second factor dealt with the role of the Democratic State Committee. Of the 130 delegates to the national convention, fifty-two were appointed by the committee. For McCarthy, this process spelled disaster. Party leaders used their appointment power to name delegates committed to Humphrey; only one of the fifty-two went to the convention committed to McCarthy. Because of party rules and the machinations of party leaders, Humphrey, who was not yet a declared candidate, grabbed more than two-thirds of the votes. Humphrey also was helped by his strong support among big-city mayors, including a large Philadelphia delegation headed by Mayor James J. Tate and Pittsburgh Mayor Joseph M. Barr, and labor leaders in the state. McCarthy's supporters and the anti-war critics were aghast that the will of the voters was systemically set aside; similar situations in other state delegations eventually led to a largely successful modification of the delegate selection rules for subsequent conventions.[44]

The 1968 Chicago Democratic convention turned out to be one of the most tumultuous conventions in American history. Anti-war activists poured into

Chicago in late August to hold demonstrations, which eventually turned into a full-scale riot. Richard J. Daley, the mayor of Chicago, overreacted first by refusing to grant parade permits and then by authorizing an overly aggressive and zealous police response to the demonstrators. The stand-off between the demonstrators and the police broke into open warfare on the night the nominations took place, with police chasing the demonstrators with mace, tear gas, and clubs.

Within the convention hall the delegates debated peace resolutions and the debate turned ugly. The issue of the Vietnam War was joined in the anti-war candidacies of McCarthy and Senator George S. McGovern of South Dakota, while the Humphrey forces wanted to continue the war policy of the Johnson administration. The dramatic high point was an exchange between Senator Abraham A. Ribicoff of Connecticut and Mayor Daley. Ribicoff interrupted his nomination speech for McGovern to taunt the mayor: "With George McGovern we wouldn't have Gestapo tactics on the streets of Chicago." Daley was furious and the television cameras caught the mayor in a screaming response, complete with epithets and obscenities.

In the end, the Humphrey forces dominated the convention and with the votes of the Pennsylvania delegation, he easily won the nomination on the first ballot. There was division within the Pennsylvania delegation, albeit from a small contingent of liberals led by Milton J. Shapp, the Democratic nominee for governor in 1966. Astoundingly Shapp, a McCarthy advocate, demonstrated with the dissidents in the streets of Chicago, protesting the manner in which the Chicago police were handling the demonstrators. Inside the convention, Humphrey chose Senator Ed Muskie of Maine as his running mate. But the disastrous convention, as Humphrey would later admit, was catastrophic for his candidacy.

The militancy of the anti-war groups in Chicago, the urban violence in the cities during the summer, the radicalism of groups on the far left, and civil rights, states' rights issues, and affirmative action spawned the law-and-order candidacy of the governor of Alabama, George Wallace. Running under the banner of the American Independent Party, he appealed to conservatives in the South but also to blue-collar working class voters in many parts of the Midwest and Northeast.

The Republican nomination was less complicated and less intense. Michigan Governor George W. Romney's promising campaign was stopped in its tracks when he did an interview with a Detroit television station on August 31, 1967, and said that he had been "brainwashed" by American officials during a visit to Saigon in 1965. Following his visit to Vietnam he had become a staunch supporter of the war, but his admission that he had been sold a bill of goods on the success of the American military situation led many, including some Republican Party leaders, to conclude that he did not have the judgment to be president. At the outset of the campaign he had the support of many governors, including two leading Pennsylvanians: former Governor Bill Scranton and current Governor Raymond P. Shafer. At the same time, an effort by California Governor Ronald W. Reagan came to naught.

The party eventually turned to its 1960 nominee, Richard Nixon. The former vice president had Pennsylvania roots. He could trace thirty-six Pennsylvania ancestors in his lineage, and his great-grandfather had been killed at the Battle of Gettysburg. From 1947 until 1954, his parents had lived in York County and his uncle Ernest, who was one of the world's leading researchers on potatoes, worked at Penn State University.[45]

Nixon had spent the time since Goldwater's disaster in 1964 currying party favor by raising money and attending Republican banquets and meetings all over the country. Additionally, he was the overwhelming choice of the Republican voters in the spring of 1968, according to the media polls, and he had the support of many state and local party leaders. Nixon was easily nominated on the first ballot.

The Democrats were in complete disarray as the fall rolled around, divided by their positions on the war in Vietnam. On September 30, Humphrey finally broke with LBJ on the war. He announced that if elected, he would halt the bombings of North Vietnam. But his campaign had taken too long to get into gear. This was clear when he arrived in Philadelphia for a post-Labor Day visit and his very small crowd gave more applause to a hometown comedian, Joey Brown. The vice president also had to contend with anti-war hecklers. Furthermore, his suggestion that some of the troops could be brought home from Vietnam in late 1968 or early 1969 drew a sharp rebuke from President Johnson. Speaking before the American Legion the next day, the president thundered that no man could make that prediction.[46]

Both Humphrey and Nixon had to deal with the third-party candidacy of Wallace, whose anti-establishment populism was aimed at the critics of the Vietnam War. The Alabamian also lodged a full-throated appeal to angry white men by criticizing welfare recipients, castigating the radical groups that had emerged in the 1960s, and opposing the racial integration of schools. Sensing that the deep division within the nation required a unity candidate, Nixon argued that he was the only candidate who could unite the country. He pledged to restore law and order and indicated that he would represent the "forgotten Americans." On the eve of the election, he announced that he had a new secret plan to end the Vietnam War; the position helped him eke out a narrow national victory.

As the campaign progressed, the Democrats began to pull together, and Humphrey surged in the polls. A mid-October Harris Poll showed him trailing Nixon by five percentage points, 40 percent to 35 percent, with Wallace at 18 percent. The surge was led in Pennsylvania by organized labor, which gave Humphrey's campaign a huge boost. The Republicans' strategy, in addition to turning out rural and suburban voters, focused on reversing their slide among Philadelphia voters. The Nixon campaign aimed to secure at least a 40 percent plurality in Philadelphia, a benchmark considered essential for a state victory. The campaign received assurance from William A. Meehan, the city Republican leader, that the goal was achievable. Republican leaders wanted Nixon to compete specifically for black voters in Philadelphia. Nixon had won 20 percent of the black vote in the city in 1960, and W. Thacher Longstreth, the head of the city's Chamber of Commerce, urged Nixon to meet privately with black leaders. Nixon refused. He argued that suburban voters would be alienated if they perceived that he was making deals with black leaders.[47]

Pennsylvania was a toss-up state right up to Election Day. The national election was, indeed, a squeaker. Nixon won 43.4 percent of the popular vote to Humphrey's 42.7 percent, or by about 500,000 votes out of 73 million cast. Wallace won almost 10 million votes. The electoral vote was better for Nixon; he won 301 to 191. Wallace won 46 electoral votes, the largest number for a third party since Theodore Roosevelt's 88 in 1912. It might be more accurate to say that Humphrey lost the election rather than Nixon won it, however. Nixon polled only a little better than Goldwater had done in 1964, but Humphrey's vote fell 13 million short of LBJ's 1964 record performance.

In Pennsylvania, Democrats united their disparate pro-war and anti-war factions sufficiently for Humphrey to carry the state. Nixon became the first Republican president in history to win the presidency without capturing Pennsylvania. Humphrey did not win a majority; he won 48 percent to Nixon's 44 percent. Humphrey won 2.26 million votes by carrying only fifteen counties, but he won by an impressive 100,000-vote majority in Allegheny. In Philadelphia the margin was 271,000 votes, more than accounting for Humphrey's 170,000-vote victory in the state. Nixon's voting pattern was close to his 1960 county totals in most of the state, and Humphrey ran a bit better than Kennedy in the Democratic regions of the southwest and the northeast.

With eight percent of the vote, Wallace's showing was not particularly impressive. A debate has ensued over whether the winner might have been different in Pennsylvania without his candidacy. A close examination of his vote indicates his candidacy made no difference in the outcome because he drew support from both Democrats and Republicans in sufficient numbers to prevent a shift to Nixon. Wallace exceeded his eight percent state average in Democratic Allegheny, Fayette, Lawrence, Washington, and Westmoreland counties, as well as in Republican Bucks, Cumberland, Dauphin, Delaware, Franklin, Fulton, Perry, and York.[48]

Pennsylvania and the Primary Election Process

Ironically, just as Pennsylvania became a competitive prize in presidential general elections, its role in the nomination of presidential candidates was virtually eliminated. This change came with the growing importance of state presidential primaries. From the first presidential nominating conventions in the 1830s until 1968, decision-making was largely in the hands of political leaders and party bosses. Because the voters played a limited role in the process, twists and turns at the conventions often led to compromise choices as factions competed for the nomination. Pennsylvania leaders were often part of the backroom negotiations and deal-making. But after 1968, the major parties changed the way in which delegates were selected to attend the conventions and the manner in which they pledged their support for prospective nominees.

Before 1972, state party primaries were of some importance, but not often definitive in the nomination for several reasons. They were few in number, starting with the first held in Wisconsin in 1905 and reaching twenty in 1972. The number of delegates sent by primary states to conventions before 1972 constituted a small percentage of the attendees. Most of those elected by voters or selected in party conventions were party activists, who largely ran officially unpledged to any particular candidate. Also, many delegates were loyal party workers who often held patronage jobs, which meant they went to conventions under the control of party leaders.

Still, from the first set of primaries held in 1905 until 1968, several did matter in the selection of presidential candidates. In 1912, there were twelve state primaries in the battle between incumbent President William Howard Taft and former President Theodore Roosevelt. Roosevelt won most of the primaries, even defeating Taft in his home state of Ohio. Roosevelt easily carried Pennsylvania, winning the lion's share of the delegates and defeating Taft by 20 percentage points, but party leaders around the country controlled the convention – in part because they had secured the votes of the delegates from non-primary states. After Taft won the nomination, Roosevelt ran on a third-party ticket. That split the Republican vote, allowing Democrat Woodrow Wilson to win the presidency. In 1952, Eisenhower and Taft battled through the primaries with Taft having the edge on delegates selected in the primaries, but unpledged delegates gave Ike the advantage. In 1960, John Kennedy's primary victories in Wisconsin and West Virginia gave him momentum, and they were crucial to his nomination. Hubert Humphrey, on the other hand, won the Democratic nomination in 1968 without entering a single primary, but all of that was about to change.

Because of rule changes adopted at the 1968 Democratic convention, and modified in subsequent conventions, party primaries came to largely determine the nominees months before the conventions. Every candidate nominated after 1968 has had to enter an expanding list of state primaries and field a slate of candidates pledged to their candidacy. The Republicans followed suit, but the modifications to their delegation selection rules have been less expansive. In 2004, the number of states holding primaries totaled thirty-five. Another important delegation selection trend made history in 2008. Many states moved their primary dates forward in the calendar, front-loading the process. By February 5, thirty states had delegate selection events – the largest number of states to select delegates that early in the presidential election calendar year in American history.

Pennsylvania conducts a closed primary, in which a voter may vote only in his or her own primary, and registered independents are not permitted to vote in party primaries. In primary elections, delegate candidates to the national conventions are permitted to run pledged or unpledged to presidential candidates. From 1913 to 1968, even though state law permitted a candidate, for example, to indicate support to a particular candidate, a delegate was not legally bound to honor the pledge. Most delegates in the earlier period, therefore, ran unpledged. Additionally, the name of the presidential candidate in this process – often called the beauty contest – appeared on a separate line on the ballot. The wishes of the delegates did not necessarily bear any relationship to the winner of the presidential beauty contest.

With a primary occurring later in the campaign season than many other states, Pennsylvania usually has been largely irrelevant in the nominating process since the 1980s despite its large number of electoral votes. The turnout in the primaries in the state has varied, but on average it was relatively low, about 15 to 20 percent of eligible voters. Undoubtedly, the low turnout related to the lack of any meaning in the vote in most primaries.

The nature of the state's electorate also has changed. Pre-primary polls taken in presidential primaries since 1972 showed that Democratic primary voters tended to be more moderate in ideology, often belonging to labor unions, and often Catholic. As a result, moderate candidates tended to do much better: Hubert Humphrey in 1972, Jimmy Carter in 1976, Walter Mondale in 1984, and Bill Clinton in 1992. Edward M. Kennedy's victory in 1980 over Carter was one exception. The polls showed a division between the more liberal and cosmopolitan southeastern counties, including Philadelphia, and the more moderate to conservative rural counties in the southwestern parts of the state.

Though the Republicans had even fewer contested Pennsylvania presidential primaries, when given alternatives they also chose the more moderate of the candidates, and often by wide margins: Gerald R. Ford over Ronald Reagan in 1976, George H. W. Bush over Reagan in 1980, Bush over Pat Robertson in 1988, and Bush over Patrick Buchanan in 1992.

Nationally between 1968 and 1972, the golden days of back-room wheeling and dealing for presidential nominations effectively came to an end. Pennsylvania's pivotal role in the presidential nomination process ended as well. With Pennsylvania's primary date remaining in late April, voters were left without a voice as presidential nominations usually wrapped up in earlier primaries.

Chapter 5
The Split Decision: the 1970s

The 1968 election demonstrated conclusively that much had changed in Pennsylvania politics over the past three decades. Most important, the state had evolved since the 1940s into one of the most competitive states in the nation. Ignored for much of the nineteenth and early parts of the twentieth century, Pennsylvania now stood at the epicenter of presidential electoral politics.

1972: Nixon and McGovern

By the beginning of 1972, the reelection of President Richard M. Nixon seemed reasonably assured. The president was winding down the Vietnam War abroad, and domestically he handled the nation's economic problems with wage and price controls that mitigated most of the economic slide until after the 1972 election. At his urging, Congress increased social welfare spending on Medicare, Medicaid, and Social Security. Nixon did not, however, obtain passage of his proposal for a guaranteed minimum income for every American family.

Concerned about his political right flank and the candidacy of George Wallace, who again sought the presidency and appealed to voters' fears about urban violence, rising crime, and the social drift to the left, Nixon championed a law-and-order approach designed to attract southerners and white conservatives. But in his quest for reelection, he engaged in activities that eventually brought about his resignation from office. He used the Internal Revenue Service to audit the tax returns of his political enemies. He also employed a secret unit to spy on his political enemies and reporters, ultimately involving the FBI and the CIA in domestic politics. Finally, he tried to cover up his reelection campaign committee's bungled effort to break into the headquarters of the National Democratic Party in the Watergate complex in Washington, D.C. The full ramifications of these activities were concealed or did not become apparent until after the 1972 election. Consequently, they had no effect on the election's outcome, despite the indictment of seven men, including two White House aides for the Watergate burglary. Meanwhile, the Wallace challenge ended when the former governor was the victim of an assassination attempt on May 15, 1972. Paralyzed from the waist down by the would-be assassin's bullet, he withdrew from the race.

The Democrats nominated the very liberal opponent of the Vietnam War, Senator George S. McGovern of South Dakota. The Senator won the nomination in part because he understood the changing delegate selection rules. He started

On a Philadelphia street, pro-labor advocates clash over their preferences in the 1972 presidential race. (Temple University Libraries, Urban Archives)

campaigning the earliest, organized in the early primary states, and raised suffi-cient campaign resources. McGovern originally had been co-chair of the commis-sion that rewrote the Democratic Party's delegate selection rules. He made good use of his knowledge, targeting delegates in a grass-roots effort that gave him a huge advantage in committed delegates on the eve of the party's national conven-tion. Of the possible Democratic nominees, McGovern not only had staked out a strong anti-Vietnam War position, but he was also the most liberal of the candi-dates. Nevertheless, he did not begin the year as the Democratic favorite to run against President Nixon. The leader in the public polls was Senator Edmund M. Muskie, the Democrats' vice presidential candidate in 1968, who started the polit-ical season by winning the New Hampshire primary. But McGovern stunned everyone with a strong second place showing; he won 38 percent to Muskie's 48 percent. The other contenders in the race were Senator Henry "Scoop" Jackson of Washington and, waiting in the wings, the old war horse Hubert H. Humphrey.

In the Pennsylvania primary, no candidate had a lock on either the voters or the political leaders. Muskie had the support of Governor Milton J. Shapp, who actively raised funds for him, and Peter J. Camiel, the powerful chairman of the

Philadelphia Democratic Party. McGovern bypassed the Keystone State to campaign in Massachusetts, which had its primary on the same day. But through a network of activists he focused his attention on winning delegates in Pennsylvania's fifty senatorial districts, a strategy that succeeded with him winning the second-largest number of delegates elected in the primary. Both Jackson and Humphrey had strong labor support, but years of a close relationship with organized labor paid more dividends for Humphrey, who garnered the endorsement of the large industrial labor organizations. He also had another advantage. He had defeated President Nixon in the state in 1968. Over the years he had developed solid working relationships with political leaders and had the experience of past campaigns. Pennsylvania was so congenial to Humphrey that he announced his candidacy for the presidency in Philadelphia, and he was not disappointed by the Pennsylvania primary results.

He carried the state with almost 482,000 popular votes, or 35 percent of the total. This was Humphrey's first primary victory, and he won it essentially by carrying the union, Catholic, working-class towns of western Pennsylvania, wining every county west of the Susquehanna River except for Centre and Union. He also demonstrated a broad geographic base; he won fifty-two of sixty-seven counties, dominating the entire state with the exception of the southeast and the northeast. Muskie won 20 percent, drawing his strongest support from six counties in the northeast, and McGovern, who also garnered 20 percent, ran strong in the four counties in the southeast. Surprisingly, George Wallace won 21 percent of the vote. In the vital delegate hunt Humphrey won 57, McGovern 37, Muskie 29, and Wallace just two. Wallace's strong popular vote did not translate into the election of many delegates because the popular presidential vote was cast separately from the delegate elections, and his delegate candidates failed to win, with two exceptions. No Republican candidate filed in the state's presidential primary other than Nixon, who locked up the sixty unpledged Republican delegates.

In the end, McGovern won the Democratic nomination with his army of anti-war activists and liberals, who packed the convention in Miami Beach with their supporters. He defeated his closest rival, Henry Jackson, 4-to-1 in the balloting. In a series of rules confrontations, the McGovernites denied convention seats to union leaders and party regulars, including the Chicago delegation headed by Mayor Richard J. Daly. In past conventions many of these leaders had been the back-room negotiators and power players, but no longer. The convention proved to be a public relations nightmare. The sessions lasted well into the night, and the debates focused on controversial social issues. Typically, presidential candidates accrue an increase in voter support after their conventions, commonly referred to as a convention bounce. But in 1972 McGovern gained no additional voter support, according to the Gallup organization.

Miami Beach also hosted the Republican convention, but other than the ease with which Nixon was nominated, the similarities ended. The president won every vote at the convention except for one cast for California Congressman Pete McCloskey. The convention was a scripted, made-for-television event. Activities inside the convention were safely in the hands of Nixon forces. Outside the hall, anti-war demonstrations were common, but they did not mar the unity or the enthusiasm of the Republican delegates. Nixon left the convention with a sizable lead over McGovern.

Among Nixon's supporters were some conservative Democrats, including the mayor of Philadelphia, the conservative former law-and-order police commissioner Frank Rizzo. Nixon and Rizzo liked each other and agreed on taking a tough approach on crime. "People react to fear, not love," Nixon had declared during his very first senatorial campaign. "They don't teach that in Sunday school, but it's true." The president had high praise for Rizzo. So it came as no shock in April 1972 when Rizzo informed Democrats in the state that he would not support McGovern.[49]

It would have been one thing for the mayor to sit on his hands and not work for McGovern, but soon Rizzo had his top aides out campaigning for Nixon. Rizzo personally wrote a strategy memo to the president, urging him to avoid any direct appeal for black votes and to concentrate on the votes of white conservative ethnics and organized labor. He also indicated his support for the president's Vietnam War policy. Although the president ran some risk in getting too publicly chummy with Rizzo, whose mayoral campaign had been racially charged, Nixon accepted the support. The mayor received confidential briefings from the Nixon campaign, and Philadelphia benefited from increased federal government largess as the Nixon administration rewarded its Philadelphia friend. The mayor's electoral goal was to keep McGovern's majority in the city below 100,000, a goal that was achieved. Nixon lost the city by 88,000 votes. Later Nixon gave Rizzo credit for helping him win reelection, especially his effort to build support among white urban ethnics.

By consensus, the McGovern campaign was a disaster. After pledging "1,000 percent" allegiance to his vice presidential running mate, Senator Thomas F. Eagleton of Missouri, he replaced him just weeks after the Democratic Convention when he learned the senator had undergone electric shock theory for depression. Perhaps more important were the deep divisions within the Democratic Party. McGovern had alienated many of his own party's leaders and organized labor with his liberal positions on welfare, drug use, and, of course, strident opposition to the Vietnam War. McGovern did not, however, modify his positions for the sake of party harmony. In late September in Philadelphia he held up a pineapple bomb and rhetorically asked whether the nation's honor increased because the color of the body count had changed from "white to yellow." "The blood is still red," he exhorted. One of his leading political opponents, Senator Hugh Scott, played off McGovern's liberal positions by calling him the "Three A candidate – acid, amnesty, and abortion."[50]

McGovern's overall approach in the campaign was to raise public awareness of the abuse of power, but he was uniformly unsuccessful. Many of the abuses eventually came to light, especially the infamous Watergate break-in of June 1972, but the full ramifications did not become apparent to many Americans until after the election. Meanwhile, just days before the election, Nixon's Secretary of State, Henry Kissinger, returned from the Paris peace negotiations with the North Vietnamese and boldly announced that peace was at hand. Politically, the announcement was dramatic and helpful to Nixon's reelection, but it was a substantial exaggeration for a war that would linger for three more years.

With a huge lead in the polls, Nixon ventured out of the White House mostly to tie his policy initiatives to the campaign. Typical was his stop in Philadelphia a few weeks before the election to sign the revenue sharing bill. The Nixon campaign raised a phenomenal $60 million in the course of the race, much of it from big corporate interests such as the Pittsburgh Mellons and the Philadelphia Annenbergs, owners of the *Philadelphia Inquirer*. Virtually every paper in the state endorsed Nixon. A notable exception was William W. Scranton 3rd, son of the former Republican governor and presidential candidate, who owned several small weekly papers that came out for McGovern.

The election results were never much in doubt. McGovern was crushed. The president won 61 percent of the national popular vote, the senator only 38 percent. Nixon won forty-nine states, while McGovern won only Massachusetts and the District of Columbia. The popular vote margin was a spectacular 18 million. The 520 to 17 electoral vote victory was historic by any comparison. But McGovern's defeat was personal. It did not translate into widespread Democratic defeats around the country or in Congress. The Republicans picked up a modest twelve seats in the House, but lost two in the Senate.

Similarly, there were no Nixon coattails in Pennsylvania despite the huge win. The Democrats won the two statewide contested row office elections. They lost control of the state House, but they maintained control of the state Senate and the congressional delegation. Nixon won sixty-six counties while McGovern could only win Philadelphia. On his way to winning almost 60 percent of the vote, Nixon increased his party's share of the presidential vote by 10 percent or more in twenty-two counties. Still, overall the election did not generate great enthusiasm among the state's voters; the turnout dropped nine percentage points from 67 percent in 1968 to 58 percent in 1972.

The 1972 election was not a watershed. No large realignment of voters took place. Democratic leaders around the state were divided but not discouraged.

Many of the liberal activists who made up the McGovern campaign were incorporated into the party in an uneasy truce. But for labor leaders, their exclusion from the McGovern campaign and the drift of the party's activists towards cultural liberalism began to alienate the conservative Democratic ethnic Catholic voters of the state. That was an ominous sign of the changes to come in subsequent elections.

1976: Ford and Carter

When Pennsylvania Governor Milton J. Shapp decided to run for the presidency in 1975, he surprised many Americans, as well as the voters of the Keystone State. No one thought he could win, and almost no one really wanted him to run, not even his wife, Muriel. Those who thought he should run indicated that he should resign as governor. He ran and did not resign – a direct contradiction of his policy of requiring his appointees to resign their state jobs if they sought elective public office.

Shapp suggested he might seek the presidency in June 1975, at the National Governors Conference in New Orleans, and formally announced in Washington on September 25. The Democrats had every reason to be optimistic about their prospects to regain the presidency. Nixon's resignation as president in August 1974 left Vice President Gerald R. Ford a caretaker president. The post-Watergate political environment and his pardon of Nixon hung like an albatross around his 1976 election effort. Personally popular, Ford enjoyed a solid reputation for honesty, and his down-home simplicity was a welcome relief from the imperial and imperious attitude that had permeated the Nixon years.

Shapp's candidacy drew little national attention and it had even less electoral success, in spite of the fact that the Democratic nomination was wide open. After a disastrous March 12 showing in the Florida primary, where he won three percent of the total vote – 6,000 fewer votes than "no preference" – Shapp withdrew from the contest. In the course of his campaign, the Pennsylvania governor visited twenty-five states and spent $850,000, about half of which was his own money. He could easily afford it. As head of Jerrold Electronics, he had made millions before becoming governor in 1970. Since his initiation into politics in 1960 as head of the "Business and Professional Men" for John Kennedy and as a member of the Democratic Party's State Executive Committee, he had been ambitious to hold elective public office. He ran and won a gubernatorial primary in 1966 as an outsider, excoriating the machine politics of his party. He lost in the general election that year, ran again in 1970, and defeated Lt. Governor Raymond J. Broderick.

The governor no doubt thought his record as a big state governor gave him ample qualifications to be president. Inheriting a nightmare of a fiscal crisis, he solved it the following year by enacting the state's first permanent flat income tax, set at 2.5 percent. The tax put the state's fiscal house in order temporarily. At the end of his first term, Shapp could boast of a string of policy successes: he expanded state employment opportunities for women, blacks, and gays; he concluded major union contracts that ended patronage to all but about 4,000 of the state's 110,000 workers; and he won legislative approval for a liberal no-fault auto insurance law. One of the most liberal governors in modern Pennsylvania history, Shapp vetoed abortion control proposals, capital punishment bills, anti-busing legislation, and proposals that would have prevented gays and lesbians from serving in the state police force or as prison guards.

But it was his success at helping settle a national independent truckers strike in February 1974 that brought him national attention. The strike was triggered when the Nixon administration imposed a fifty-miles-per-hour speed limit on interstate highways and restricted the fuel supplies of truckers. The strike led to violence against non-strikers on Pennsylvania's interstates and elsewhere, caus-

Governor Milton J. Shapp greets the crowd and television cameras outside the Bellevue-Strafford hotel in Philadelphia. While initially seeking the 1976 Democratic nomination, Shapp eventually left the race and pledged to vote for opponent Jimmy Carter on the first ballot at the party convention. (Temple University Libraries, Urban Archives)

ing Shapp to call out the National Guard. Shapp realized that the independent truckers had legitimate concerns, however, and he went to Washington and initially persuaded the federal government and the representatives of the striking truckers to work out a moratorium and then a final settlement of the disputed issues. Flush with success, Shapp no doubt believed he had the credentials to seek the presidency.

Yet Shapp's quixotic presidential bid destroyed his second term. In a deal roundly condemned, especially by Shapp's liberal friends, he made an arrangement with his political nemesis Philadelphia Mayor Frank Rizzo for the thirty national convention delegates the mayor controlled. The deal was simple: Shapp acquired the votes and the mayor obtained Shapp's support to oust the current head of the Philadelphia Democratic City Committee in favor of a Rizzo man. The city also secured Shapp's legislative support for a 29 percent real estate tax hike. The liberal Shapp and the conservative Nixon-supporting mayor constructed an old-fashioned, opportunistic deal. Politically, Shapp never recovered from the criticism. And it was not for lack of trying. After Jimmy Carter won the Democratic nomination, Shapp campaigned so vigorously for the Georgian that he ruptured a blood vessel in his throat.[51]

In the main contest for the Democratic nomination, the success of Carter was itself surprising. Having served only a single term as governor of Georgia, an unlikely state to send forth a Democratic nominee in the post-1960 era, Carter ran as the consummate outsider against the politically corrupt system that had produced Watergate. He promised to restore trust and confidence in the federal government. His smart and aggressive campaign paid dividends early in the nomination process when he won almost all the early primaries, knocking down some old faces, such as Henry Jackson and George Wallace, and some new faces, such as Senators Fred R. Harris of Oklahoma and Birch E. Bayh of Indiana, as well as Congressman Morris K. Udall of Arizona.

After Shapp withdrew from the race, it was open season in Pennsylvania with the contenders having free rein to seek endorsements and voter support. The contest in the state highlighted Carter and two other candidates, Jackson and Udall. The liberals in the party galvanized around Udall while many party regulars, including Mayor Rizzo and Philadelphia Democratic City Chairman Peter Camiel and labor leaders, supported Jackson. Surprising almost everyone, the liberal Shapp threw his support to the conservative Jackson, but nothing could stop a Carter primary victory in the state. For Jackson a victory in Pennsylvania was essential to keep his flagging national campaign viable. In Pittsburgh maverick Mayor Peter F. Flaherty endorsed Carter. At a press conference with Flaherty on April 21, Carter condemned the politics-as-usual practices in the nation, including the extensive use of patronage – a not very subtle reference to the patronage practices still employed in the state. Carter named names, criticizing Rizzo and

In 1976, President Gerald Ford enjoys a campaign stop at South Philadelphia's Italian Market. (Library of Congress)

asserting he would not have accepted Rizzo's endorsement under any circumstances. In Philadelphia two days later, Carter continued the criticism while stumping in the mayor's home town.

Carter won the Pennsylvania primary with more than 500,000 votes, or 37 percent of the total. Jackson was second with 25 percent, and Udall third with 19 percent. Carter won 64 of the contested delegates elected out of the state's senate districts to Udall's 22 and Jackson's 19. Though out of the race, Shapp won 17 delegates. Carter was able to build a broad coalition in the state. Except for Philadelphia, Carter won every region of the state, and he did well among blue-collar workers despite organized labor's efforts on behalf of Jackson. He notably won the ethnic region of Scranton and Wilkes-Barre, and he even carried the Philadelphia suburbs.

The Pennsylvania primary was important nationally because it virtually secured the nomination for Carter and eliminated Jackson from the contest. Two days after the primary, Humphrey, waiting in the wings for a deadlocked convention and realizing the Pennsylvania victory made the Georgian's march to the nomination unstoppable, announced he would not be a candidate in 1976.

In the Republican contest, President Ford was the front runner for the nomination by the time of the Pennsylvania primary in April. His principal opponent nationally, Ronald Reagan, did not contest the state. The entire Republican establishment in the Commonwealth lined up behind Ford, including both Republican U.S. senators, ten of thirteen Republican congressmen, and the vast majority of the state's Republican elected officials. Under these circumstances and considering Reagan's no-show status, the Republican convention delegation was overwhelmingly committed to Ford.

Nationally the Republican picture was very different; the campaign between Ford and Reagan was brutal and went down to wire. Reagan had inherited the Goldwater mantle. By comparison, Ford was more moderate and certainly more pragmatic. In a dramatic effort to move moderates and uncommitted convention delegates his way, Reagan named his vice presidential running mate before the opening of the Republican convention. He chose moderate Pennsylvania U.S. Senator Richard S. Schweiker. While representing Montgomery County in the House of Representatives, Schweiker had won a U.S. Senate seat in 1968 when he defeated liberal icon Joseph Clark. As Republicans were losing in droves in the post-Watergate 1974 election, he won reelection over Pittsburgh Mayor Peter Flaherty. Even before the August 1974 impeachment process began, Schweiker had inoculated himself against the charge that he had been a Nixon man by calling for the president's resignation. He was aided in his reelection by considerable campaign assistance from organized labor.

Reagan's goal in selecting a running mate was to balance the ticket, and he thought with Schweiker he might move some uncommitted northern delegates. The senator's record seemed to confirm the wisdom of Reagan's decision. Schweiker had voted to override numerous Nixon vetoes, and he had voted against two of the president's Supreme Court nominees. Additionally, he had very high legislative ratings from organized labor and liberal activist groups. Schweiker and Reagan held a six-hour meeting to discuss the nomination plan, but there was simply too little time before the convention and too little inclination among delegates to change the outcome of the nomination struggle. Plus, the Reagan campaign underestimated the backlash among conservative Republicans who thought the arrangement untenable. Schweiker's main reason for accepting Reagan's offer was his contention that he could help bridge the ideological differences within the party. Naturally, his critics saw it differently. They believed he had surrendered his principles for the opportunity to become vice president. Ironically, Schweiker had actually approached Ford about joining his ticket before the entreaty from Reagan, giving some credence to the accusation that the senator was motivated by ambition for the vice presidency.

The prospect of Schweiker's nomination as Reagan's running mate did not weaken support for Ford within the Pennsylvania delegation. At the Kansas City convention, the delegates held firm for Ford. Former Governor Scranton and Senator Scott joined other Republican leaders in opposing the early announcements of running mates. They claimed this position on the principle of the matter and not because they opposed Schweiker's candidacy. But during an address to the Pennsylvania delegation, Scranton shocked the delegates when he indicated he would accept the vice presidential nomination if offered to him. One reason he made himself available was to lock in votes for Ford among uncommitted members of the Pennsylvania delegation, which certainly weakened the Reagan-Schweiker ticket.[53]

In the end, the vice presidential offer to Schweiker made no difference because Ford edged out Reagan on the first ballot, 1,187 to 1,070. He named conservative Kansas Senator Robert J. Dole as his running mate. For Schweiker, 1976 was a watershed year. He turned sharply to the right politically, notably casting votes against big labor in the Senate. The 1976 episode also ended his national career. Conservatives would not trust him, and moderates never forgave his embrace of Reagan. In 1979, he announced he would not seek a third Senate term; his national ambitions fell silent.

Realizing the importance and the competitiveness of Pennsylvania, Ford and Carter spent considerable time in the state, especially during the final weeks of the campaign. They sent their vice presidential candidates into the state as well. Four years earlier McGovern had a divided Pennsylvania Democratic Party; in 1976 Carter did not. Even Mayor Rizzo in Philadelphia was now on board, promising to deliver Philadelphia by a huge majority. He did, and Carter needed every vote he could get in the city to carry the state.

The general election campaign was not particularly inspiring. Carter held a lead throughout the fall. Ford adopted the Rose Garden strategy and stayed close to the White House, appearing presidential. The strategy almost worked. Neither candidate captured the imagination of the voters. In fact, turnout was the lowest since the 1948 election.

The candidates debated three times, in a restoration of an event that became a staple of presidential campaigns thereafter. Ford had to deal with a stumbling economy – rising inflation and unemployment – and the unpopularity of his decision to pardon former President Nixon. Given the domestic problems confronting the nation, Carter's victory was surprisingly small; he won a bit more than 50 percent of the popular vote, and Ford won 48 percent. Carter was only the third Democrat to win a majority of the popular vote since the Civil War. His electoral vote majority was decisive, winning by 56 votes, 297 to 241. Carter's southern roots were important in his victory; he won the old Confederacy, except Virginia, and most of the states east of the Mississippi. For the most part, Ford won the western states. The Democrats retained their large post-Watergate majorities in Congress.

Carter carried Pennsylvania by 123,000 votes – a razor-thin 50 to 48 per-cent margin, identical to his national percentage. As promised, Rizzo in an unusu-al alliance with the black leaders and other anti-Rizzo Democrats in the city pro-duced a 256,000-vote victory for the Georgia governor. Carter won twenty-one counties, the usual Democratic strongholds in the northeast and southwest. In the four suburban Philadelphia counties, Ford held his own among the Republican voters, but he did not do as well as expected in rural central Pennsylvania. As befit-ting the closeness of the race, nineteen counties had an election winner with 53 percent of the vote or less.

1976 Democratic nominee Jimmy Carter addresses the crowd during a campaign stop in Pittsburgh. While Carter eventually carried Pennsylvania in the election, his slim margin of victory reflected the growing competitiveness of the state. (Library of Congress)

Chapter 6

The New Political Order: the 1980s

Through the 1970s, new forces were at work transforming the political order created by the New Deal. At the national level, the drift of the Democratic Party to the left, especially the opposition to the Vietnam War, the extension of civil rights, and the growing liberalism of its leaders in the North on social issues, began to move white southern voters into the ranks of the Republican Party. In the North, the drift caused the Democrats to lose support among ethnic voters, especially Catholics. In Pennsylvania, the losses were first noticeable in the ring of old industrial counties surrounding Allegheny County and other counties in the southwest. In practical terms, Republicans benefited greatly because they picked up Catholic, ethnic defectors in the southwest while continuing to hold onto their middle-class, educated base in the suburban southeast. Another important trend was the rise of the "New Right," an amalgam of social conservative groups energized by their opposition to abortion rights, school busing, the Equal Rights Amendment, and their perception that the courts had become too soft on criminals. These trends assisted Ronald Reagan and George H. W. Bush, who carried the state's electoral votes in three straight presidential elections beginning in 1980.

1980: Carter and Reagan

During his 1980 reelection year, President Jimmy Carter was beset with innumerable domestic and international problems. None was more important than the Iranian hostage crisis, in which Iranian Islamic radicals held fifty-three Americans hostage in Teheran, ultimately for 444 days but during the entire duration of the presidential campaign. At home, the economy cost Carter substantial support from his Democratic blue-collar base. Inflation rose to 13 percent at the beginning of the election year, and oil prices, pushed up by OPEC, reached $30 per barrel, and Americans saw gas at the pumps rise to almost one dollar per gallon. Carter's response was to go on national television, wearing a cardigan sweater, and tell the American people that the era of cheap energy was over and with it their modern lifestyles. These admonitions did not increase his popularity and endangered his reelection, especially when he was matched up against the likely Republican nominee, the buoyant, optimistic Ronald Reagan.

Unhappiness with Carter carried over to the liberal wing of his own party. He faced an immediate and serious challenge from his party's liberal champion, Massachusetts Senator Edward M. Kennedy. Carter won ten of the thirteen primaries held prior to Pennsylvania's, but fully one-third of the voters failed to support him. The president refused to campaign personally in the primaries, citing the hostage situation, and he was no doubt aided by the resurfacing of stories about Kennedy's behavior in 1969 when he fled a Chappaquiddick, Massachusetts, car accident in which a young woman drowned.

By the mid-April Pennsylvania primary, Carter had won 54 percent of the primary popular vote and 63 percent of the delegates selected up to that time. In many respects, that made Pennsylvania a do-or-die state for Kennedy, who campaigned heavily. He toured the state in a fourteen-day nonstop marathon, leaving virtually no part of the state untouched by his frenzied activity. He harshly condemned Carter's handling of the economy and foreign policy. Conversely, Carter used television and relied on support from most of the party leaders and a field organization put together by his supporters. Organized labor, always a key element in Democratic politics, was badly split. Kennedy had the support of many of Philadelphia's political leaders. Carter had fourteen national unions behind him, Kennedy had twenty-one, and many of their respective state affiliates were hard at work. Further illustrating the complexity and division of union support, the president had the powerful Pennsylvania State Education Association while Kennedy had the Pennsylvania Federation of Teachers.

The Pennsylvania primary was a cliff hanger. Kennedy eked out a narrow victory, 46.2 percent to 45.6 percent, or by a less than 5,000 votes. The victory netted the Massachusetts senator 93 delegates to Carter's 92. Kennedy won only nine of sixty-seven counties, but his strong showing in Philadelphia and its suburbs and in the old coal-mining regions in the northeast made his victory possible. The key to his Philadelphia victory was in part the strong backing he received from Mayor William J. Green 3rd and the city Democratic organization. The CBS Exit Poll captured the mood of the electorate on primary day. Voters who ranked the economy and inflation the most important issues cast votes for Kennedy, while the character issue, raised by Carter in television ads in the closing days of the campaign, was cited by those who voted for Carter.[55]

By the time the national convention in New York approached, Kennedy was arithmetically eliminated and tried a new stratagem. He called for an open convention, offering to release his delegates if the president would do the same. Kennedy hoped to open the possibility that a debate over the nomination and a more liberal platform would keep his candidacy alive, but the president did not fall into the trap. Without the open convention and without the nomination votes in hand, Kennedy withdrew before the formal vote on the nomination. He endorsed Carter, but only after an electrifying speech that sparked a fifty-minute demonstration. Most of Kennedy's delegates voted for him anyway, but Carter won by a two-to-one margin. Befitting the closeness of the state's primary, the Pennsylvania delegation voted 95 to 90 for Carter. Kennedy had the hearts of the delegates, but

Carter had the nomination. Pennsylvania Democratic leaders left the convention reasonably united after a strong effort by the Carter team.

For the Republicans, the likely nominee as the Pennsylvania primary approached in mid-April was Ronald Reagan, the runner-up to Gerald Ford in 1976. Reagan's main opponent was George H. W. Bush, and Bush desperately needed a victory in the state to have any chance of capturing the nomination. Reagan had won eleven of the first fourteen primaries. Bush stumped the state and tried to draw important distinctions between himself and Reagan, notably appealing to moderate Republican audiences. He criticized Reagan on three fronts: the Californian's $210 billion tax cut proposal, his opposition to the Equal Rights Amendment, and his proposal to require states to administer the nation's welfare

Republican candidate Ronald Reagan greets supporters at a rally in Upper Darby. In both the 1980 and 1984 elections, Reagan carried Pennsylvania, due in part to his success among some of the state's traditionally Democratic voters. (Temple University Libraries, Urban Archives)

During the 1980 primary season, George H.W. Bush addresses supporters outside Independence Hall. (Temple University Libraries, Urban Archives)

proposals. His television commercials were widely considered effective. They consisted of four "Ask George Bush" telecasts, a format with live audiences asking questions to the candidate.

Republican leaders divided their allegiance. On the one hand, former Senator Richard S. Schweiker, Reagan's 1976 choice for vice president, stood with Reagan as did powerful Philadelphia Republican City Chairman Bill Meehan and Drew Lewis, a future Reagan cabinet choice. On the other hand, Bush had in his corner Elsie Hillman, a member of the National Republican Committee and a significant leader in the western part of the state, and former Senator Hugh Scott. Reagan chose to campaign elsewhere around the country, ignoring the Keystone State except for a total of four days. One of them was a single appearance the day before the primary in Lancaster, when he opposed any federal commitment to bail out Metropolitan Edison for the cleanup of the crippled Three Mile Island nuclear plant. Yet in the primary he received 525,000 votes, losing to Bush by 100,000, an impressive showing considering that Reagan spent only $100,000 compared to Bush's $1 million.

By May, the Republican contest was over. Reagan had a clear majority, and his public campaigning had made him the choice of rank-and-file Republicans. Throughout the Detroit convention the Reagan forces presented a moderate, even non-ideological face as they attempted to heal any difference with moderate Republicans. After his easy first-ballot victory, Reagan considered and then rejected a kind of co-presidency "dream ticket" with Gerald Ford as his running mate. His choice of Bush was popular, if not exciting. Choosing Bush was expected to help the ticket in some eastern states, notably Pennsylvania.

The fall campaign was especially nasty and personal. Carter called Reagan a dangerous radical and a war monger. Reagan appeared genial and unthreatening, and in their only debate he came across as calm and reflective – not at all a danger to start a nuclear war. Reagan hammered away at what he claimed was the military weakness of the country and the ineffectiveness of Carter's policies on the hostage crisis, the Strategic Arms Limitation Treaty (SALT II), and Soviet aggression. But the president's more serious problem was the economy at home.

Both campaigns zeroed in on a big-state strategy. That meant personally campaigning and spending their resources in five big targeted states: Pennsylvania as well as Ohio, Illinois, Florida, and Texas. Reagan planned to campaign in the targeted states with ninety-five major appearances in the forty-nine days between September 15 and Election Day. These key states represented 121 of the 270 electoral votes necessary to elect a president. In 1980 Pennsylvania had the third-largest number of electoral votes.[56]

By the end of the first week in October, Reagan had opened a substantial lead in Pennsylvania, 40 percent to 33 percent, while John B. Anderson, an independent candidate, trailed with 16 percent, according to the Pennsylvania Poll. The poll confirmed what most national polls were showing: that the economic woes of the country had become the principal concern of voters. In addition, Reagan was cleaning up in the vote-rich Philadelphia suburbs and doing better than expected among blue-collar, Catholic voters in the old industrial sector in the southwestern part of the state. These voters became the northern component of what would later be called the Reagan Democrats.

Going into the final weeks of the campaign, the contest tightened, but Reagan's debate performance proved significant. He asked a simple question that resonated widely: "Are you better off today than you were four years ago?" Additionally, Carter was hurt by the Iranian hostage-keepers' decision to not release their captives during the campaign. Most historians believe that Carter lost the election more than Reagan won it. Reagan defeated Carter handily by more than eight million popular votes, but he still only won 51 percent of the popular vote. Carter accumulated 41 percent of the total, and the independent candidate Anderson captured 7 percent. Reagan's electoral-vote victory was more decisive and impressive, 489 to 49. Reagan swept virtually the entire country, losing only five states and the District of Columbia. The Republicans regained the U.S. Senate for the first time since 1954 and made impressive gains in the House. This was clearly an election with coattails.

The Reagan victory in Pennsylvania was similar to the national outcome. He pushed 50 percent of the vote to Carter's 42 percent, but his edge in the popular vote was a convincing 324,000. The president managed to win only ten counties: the Democratic counties in the southwest, Lackawanna in the northeast, and Philadelphia. An impressive percentage of Democratic voters deserted Carter; according to the ABC Exit Poll, he won only 65 percent of their vote while Reagan picked up 88 percent of the Republican vote. Despite being the self-proclaimed conservative candidate, Reagan won not only 72 percent of conservatives, but 37 percent of liberal voters as well. Women voters broke 56 percent to 35 percent for Reagan, as did men 56 percent to 32 percent. Catholic voters, an important swing group, went for the California governor 48 percent to 40 percent for Carter.

1984: Reagan and Mondale

After the 1980 election, President Reagan initiated what historians refer to as the "Reagan Revolution." He argued that in the years before his presidency, the government had caused many of the nation's problems. Specifically, he wanted less regulation of the marketplace, a large tax reduction, and cutbacks on domestic programs. Some economists argued that these policies carried out by Reagan in his first term caused subsequent large federal deficits and posed a danger to safety-net programs for the poor. Others maintained that they stimulated the economic growth that took place after the 1982 recession.

The 1982 economic downturn was the most damaging recession since the Great Depression, and it hit Pennsylvania hard, especially the manufacturing sector that continued its post-World War II decline. The recession almost caused Republican Governor Richard Thornburgh – arguably the state's most important Republican – to lose his bid for reelection. After riding a wave of popularity because of his calm, reassuring leadership in the midst of the Three Mile Island

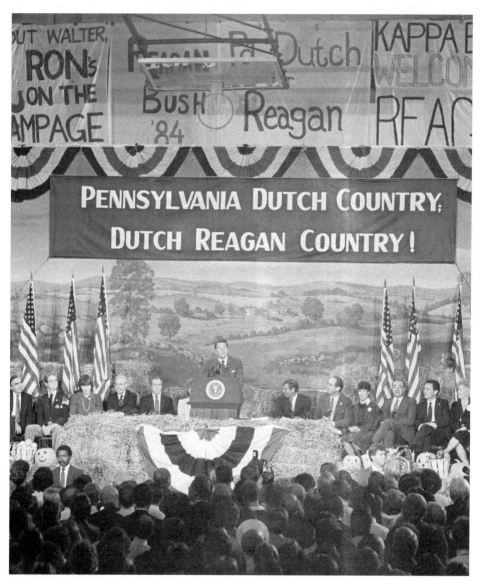

Backed by scenes of Pennsylvania farm land, "Dutch Reagan" appeals to voters in a filled Pucillo Gymnasium at Millersville University during the last days of the 1984 campaign. (Photograph by Richard Hertzler, Lancaster *New Era*)

nuclear reactor disaster, Thornburgh felt the wrath of recession-plagued voters. In 1982, he narrowly won reelection by a scant 100,000 votes against a little-known, underfinanced Democratic congressman, Allen E. Ertel.

By 1984, Reagan was riding a wave of popularity as the economy rebounded. Inflation declined to a great extent because of a drop in oil prices, the jobless rate fell, and interest rates plummeted. The president also had survived an assassination attempt in 1981, handling it with an aplomb that Americans admired. Reagan continued to radiate optimism about the American dream, confident in the future and firm in a belief in individual liberty. Reaganism, as it came to be called, appealed especially to young people and to social conservatives.

Reagan waited until January 29, after a stunning 97 percent victory in the Iowa caucus, to declare formally for a second term. Using national television to make his announcement, the president kicked off his reelection with his usual upbeat assessment of the future. "America is back and standing tall," he remarked. He sailed to renomination. Recent history has been kind to presidents who have won renomination without bitter internecine fights for a second term, and 1984 proved to be no different.[57]

The search for a Democratic opponent, meanwhile, turned into a bruising series of primary battles. The Democratic primary season seemed at the outset to favor former Carter Vice President Walter F. Mondale. He had two main rivals as the campaign progressed: Gary Hart, a reform-minded U.S. senator from Colorado, and civil rights leader Jesse Jackson. Mondale had the support of party regulars and labor leaders. He looked like an easy nomination winner, but the voters in the early primaries had a different view. Mondale and Hart battled each other indecisively in the early primaries. One of the nation's most visible and controversial black leaders, Jackson dominated the vote among black constituencies, winning large percentages in Chicago and New York City. As the Pennsylvania primary approached, Jackson threatened to chip away at Mondale's Philadelphia support.

Before the Pennsylvania primary, twelve states had voted; Hart won seven and Mondale five – though Mondale had the delegate lead. Pennsylvania followed the April New York primary by one week. New York and Pennsylvania were important primaries, sending the second- and fourth-largest numbers of delegates, respectively, to the nominating convention.

Organized labor was particularly energetic in the primary and played a significant role in the outcome in Pennsylvania. Its leaders were solidly behind Mondale because of his support for trade protection. Labor organization leaders, led by the American Federation of State, County, and Municipal Employees, the Pennsylvania State Education Association, and the AFL-CIO, began a two-week blitz of the state just prior to the April 10 primary, attempting to motivate their 1.2 million members to support the former vice president. Mondale also was the featured speaker at the AFL-CIO's state spring convention. In addition, he had the strong support of major party leaders, including a trio of Philadelphia elected officials: the African American Mayor W. Wilson Goode, former Mayor Bill Green, and District Attorney Edward G. Rendell.

Before the primary season started in earnest, Ohio Democratic Senator and former astronaut John Glenn generated some interest in the state. Two former governors, Milton Shapp and George Leader, both considered liberal, and one former mayor, Pete Flaherty of Pittsburgh, who was considered conservative, backed Glenn. At this time, almost half of the Democratic county chairmen stood behind Glenn. Though he remained on the Pennsylvania ballot, by the April primary he was no longer a viable national candidate. Thereafter, the contest turned into a three-candidate affair: Mondale, Hart, and Jackson. The three recognized the importance of the state and campaigned heavily in Pennsylvania. All three met for a debate in Pittsburgh during the last week of the campaign. In one of the more dramatic moments in the campaign, Mondale appeared on April 9 in Middletown, against the backdrop of the cooling towers at Three Mile Island, and pledged that the nuclear reactor would never open if he were elected president.[58]

Mondale won statewide, convincingly, 47 percent to Hart's 35 percent; Jackson came in third at 17 percent. Mondale's greatest strength came from the western part of the state where he decisively defeated all challengers, and he finished second to Jackson in Philadelphia. Hart ran well among middle-class, white-collar, politically moderate suburban voters. As expected, Jackson performed well in Philadelphia, winning 38 percent of the city vote, about the same as the percentage of black voters in the Quaker City. Of course, it was the important hunt for delegate votes that mattered most. Mondale won less than 50 percent of the popular votes, but 70 percent of the delegates elected in the primary had pledged support to him.

At the Democratic convention in San Francisco, Mondale won a convincing first-ballot nomination. After briefly considering, among others, Philadelphia Mayor Goode, he made history by naming a woman, three-term Congresswoman Geraldine A. Ferraro of New York, as his running mate. Unfortunately for the Democrats, Mondale damaged his own campaign right from the start with his emphasis on the need for new taxes, never a popular position. "Let's tell the truth," he announced in his acceptance speech, "Mr. Reagan will raise taxes and so will I. He won't tell you. I just did." A few weeks later the ticket was damaged further when it was revealed that Ferraro had consistently failed to disclose all her family's financial holdings during her tenure in Congress. Ferraro quickly went from being a political asset to a liability.

Reagan continued to express his sense of unbridled optimism about America's greatness. In one of the most scripted presidential campaigns in

American history, replete with the extensive use of TV emphasizing patriotic themes, Reagan easily defeated Mondale.

The size of the victory was impressive in both the popular and electoral votes. Reagan won 59 percent of the popular and 525 electoral votes. Mondale won 41 percent, and his 13 electoral votes were procured by winning one state, Minnesota, and the District of Columbia. This massive victory by Reagan did not produce any change in Congress, however; the Democrats retained control of the House and the Republicans the Senate.

Reagan increased his 1980 Pennsylvania edge, but not significantly; he won 53 percent of the vote and Mondale 46 percent. Again the county pattern was similar to four years earlier. Reagan did slightly better in the northeast, winning Lackawanna and central parts of the state, but he lost the southwest to Mondale. Mondale won only Philadelphia in the east, but he carried Allegheny and seven other counties in the western part of the state. The 1984 election results in the southwest demonstrated the nagging effects of the 1982 recession in that region.

Once again the ABC Exit Poll provides context to the popular vote totals. Reagan did better among his party's voters than did his opponent, winning 87 percent of Republicans to 80 percent of Democrats for Mondale. However, Mondale won Catholic voters narrowly, 53 percent to 47 percent. But an important income divide in the vote existed, consistent with the class appeals made during the campaign. Mondale won the income groups below $30,000 while Reagan won the groups with higher incomes, and the labor union vote was captured by Mondale 62 percent to Reagan's 38 percent. Reagan's ability to win 20 percent of the Democratic vote, along with a sizable Catholic vote and nearly 40 percent of the union vote, showed the importance of the Reagan Democrats in Pennsylvania.

1988: Bush and Dukakis

Reagan's second term was very much a mixed bag of successes and failures. In 1986, "Iran-Contra" broke and the ensuing scandal posed a serious challenge for the administration. In brief, Iran-Contra involved selling arms to Iran for the purpose of securing the release of hostages held in Lebanon by Iranian-aided terrorists. The profits from the sale were then used to provide arms to the administration-supported Contra rebels in Nicaragua – something Congress had forbidden the president to do. Throughout a nationally televised congressional investigation of what was clearly a violation of federal law, Reagan avoided any direct implication, but the revelations damaged the administration. Reagan regained his popularity by the end of his term principally because he used summits with the Soviet Union to help establish a new and profound relationship with the communist government. Internally, the Soviet Union went through fundamental changes that led to its collapse and finally to the end of the Cold War.

The Republicans began the 1988 presidential campaign optimistic about the possibility of winning three consecutive presidential elections, a feat they had not accomplished since the 1920s. The logical choice to succeed Reagan was Vice President Bush, despite the fact that no sitting vice president during the twentieth century had won election to the Oval Office. Bush had spent eight years dutifully defending the policies of the Reagan administration, but conservatives remembered the moderate Bush who had campaigned against Reagan in 1980. Particularly clear in their memories was his characterization, during the 1980 campaign, of Reagan's domestic fiscal program as "voodoo economics." As a result, he drew two conservative opponents as his main rivals for the nomination: Kansas Senator Bob Dole and television minister Pat Robertson. Nevertheless, Bush soon began wrapping up the endorsements of party leaders and elected officials.

By the time the April 26 Pennsylvania primary rolled around, Bush was the clear favorite to win the nomination. The contest settled into a two-way battle between Bush and Dole, each wooing conservative voters. Bush's advantages as vice president were too much for Dole to overcome; Bush had won sixteen primaries by mid-March. The senator withdrew on March 28, leaving only Robertson in the race. Consequently, the Pennsylvania primary was largely an irrelevant event. Bush won 79 percent of the vote to 12 percent for Robertson. On the eve of the Keystone state primary, more than 75 percent of the contested convention delegates were committed to the vice president.

Accepting his first-ballot victory at the Republican convention, Bush appealed to his party's conservatives with an acceptance speech that talked tough on terrorism, pledged economy in government, and was highlighted with a dramatic line that has been widely quoted since: "Read my lips, no new taxes."

At the outset of the presidential campaign, the Democratic race was wide open. With no incumbent, the Democrats fielded a large slate of nominees. Seven Democrats led the field: Gary Hart, who had run in 1984, Massachusetts Governor Michael S. Dukakis, House Majority Leader Richard A. Gephardt, the Reverend Jesse Jackson, and Senators Paul M. Simon of Illinois, Albert A. Gore Jr. of Tennessee, and Joseph R. Biden Jr. of Delaware. Biden was a Pennsylvania native, born in Scranton into an Irish Catholic family in 1942, the eldest of four siblings. His mother, Catherine Finnegan, was a native of Scranton, but the family left the city during the senator's childhood and moved to New Castle, Delaware. In 1972 he began a long career of service in the U.S. Senate. In January 1988, Biden's presidential campaign was dealt a lethal blow, and he withdrew from the race after allegations surfaced that he had plagiarized a speech from British Labor leader Neil Kinnock.

The front runner, Gary Hart, also found himself in difficulty and withdrew after admitting to an extramarital affair. Dukakis soon pulled ahead of the crowd as the primary season moved into high gear. He was the only one of the contenders to win a primary in every region of the country. As the Pennsylvania primary drew near, Dukakis seemed the candidate to beat. He won the New York and Wisconsin primaries decisively. By the time of the Pennsylvania primary, he had captured 30 percent of the overall votes and 34 percent of the delegates, with Jackson trailing but still in the hunt. The civil rights leader had earned 28 percent of the popular vote and 27 percent of the delegates. By mid-April, Gore, Gephardt, and Simon withdrew from the race.

Despite his lead, Dukakis took no chances. He campaigned in the state by train, traveling the 114 miles from Pittsburgh to Altoona and doing stops in between. Along the way, he targeted Bush, criticizing the vice president for ignoring the plight of the working class. In visits to Johnstown and Altoona, he stressed the need to modernize the nation's transportation infrastructure, increase the minimum wage, enact universal heath care, and restore the steel industry to its previous importance in the economy. The Massachusetts governor's campaign stops in western Pennsylvania were intended in part to halt any growth in support for Jackson among the labor voters by blunting the appeal of the minister's populist, anti-management rhetoric.

The Democratic governor of the Pennsylvania, Robert P. Casey, remained neutral and endorsed no candidate, and the Democratic State Committee, taking its cue from the governor, formally took no stand and left the candidates to fend for themselves. But other Democrats divided their support in two important ways. The vast majority of political leaders and party activists, as well as the private and public sector union leaders, backed Dukakis while African American leaders such as Philadelphia Mayor Wilson Goode supported Jackson. But to carry the state, Jackson needed to develop a substantial base of support outside of the urban southeast – something he ultimately was unable to do. Conversely, Dukakis appealed to conservative ethnic voters in the western part of the state, and he gained high-profile endorsements of Democratic leaders there, such as popular Pittsburgh Mayor Richard S. Caliguiri.

On primary day, April 26, the election outcome was very one-sided; Dukakis won 67 percent to Jackson's 28 percent. Still, Jackson was able to attract some white voters. According to the CBS News Exit Poll, Jackson won 14 percent of the white vote and a huge share of the black vote, defeating Dukakis among African Americans by a stunning 95 percent to three percent.

The lopsided popular vote victory translated into an even more one-sided delegate vote advantage. Dukakis won 167 delegates to Jackson's 11. As a result of the Pennsylvania primary, Dukakis had more than enough delegate votes locked up to confirm his status as the Democratic front runner, and he was virtually assured the nomination.

By any objective indicator, the 1988 campaign was a rough-and-tumble event. The campaign featured a torrent of negative ads and other tactics. Simply put, the Republicans tried to make Dukakis appear incompetent, weak on defense, and soft on crime. In return, the Democrats argued that the economy was weak and that Republican tax policies favored the rich and produced what Dukakis called a "Swiss-cheese economy." He appealed to pocketbook issues that resonated with voters in Pennsylvania – attracting jobs, reindustrializing the economy, and improving education. By 1988 the Pennsylvania economy was strong in the eastern part of the state, but still weak in the west, especially in the old steel and manufacturing counties in the southwest.

Throughout the campaign, Dukakis failed to define himself and seemed unable to respond to the Republican assault on his record as governor of Massachusetts. Four instances were used to great effect by the Bush campaign and left indelible impressions in the minds of many voters. The first was the widespread knowledge that Dukakis had vetoed legislation requiring public school teachers to lead their classes in the pledge of allegiance. Republicans argued the veto showed the governor's lack of patriotism. The second was the airing of the television ad showing Dukakis in a military tank wearing a helmet and looking like a turtle. The ad made the governor look silly, since he appeared to look like a child playing with a toy. The third was the revelation that Willie Horton, a convicted murderer, had raped and murdered a woman in Maryland while on release from the Dukakis weekend-furlough program. The fourth and maybe the most damaging blow came during a nationally televised debate when the moderator asked Dukakis whether, if his wife were raped and murdered, he would support an irrevocable death penalty for the killer. Dukakis's response was tepid and unemotional, and he defended his opposition to the death penalty. In varying degrees, these factors skillfully used by the Bush campaign doomed Dukakis to defeat.[59]

On the eve of the election, the national polls showed Bush with a lead but with the race tightening. Gallup had Bush ahead 53 to 41 percent, ABC-*Washington Post*, 54 to 44 percent, and CBS, 51 to 42 percent. Several other polls had the race a bit closer. As many as one in five voters were still undecided.

In the end, Bush prevailed largely because he was perceived as a surrogate for Reagan, a stand-in candidate for a president unable to seek a third term. Voters responded by indicating a strong desire to continue the policies of the Reagan administration. The nation was at peace and the economy was growing – two recipes for retaining incumbents. The vice president won 54 percent of the popular vote and 40 states. Dukakis managed only ten states, and they were located in the Northeast, the upper Midwest, and the Pacific Northwest. His 46 percent of the popular vote was respectable, but his 112 electoral votes, 29 percent of the total, were more lopsided.

In Pennsylvania, Reagan's policies had been embraced by Republican voters and leaders alike; they agreed with the president's economic prescription of lowering taxes to promote economic expansion, slowing government growth, and reducing the regulatory burden on business. The state Republican chairman, Earl

Baker, summarized the conversion succinctly: "Pennsylvania Republicans are no longer identified with the party's liberal wing as they were twenty years ago under former Governor William Scranton and former Senator Hugh Scott."[60]

The Reagan years certainly seemed congenial to Pennsylvania voters, and in return they handed the Republicans their third straight presidential victory – though narrowly so. In a contest that drew 52 percent of eligible voters to the polls, the vice president won in another nail-biter, 51 percent to Dukakis's 48 percent, earning the state's 25 electoral votes. The majority of the fifteen counties Dukakis carried had been won by Democrats since 1976. The closeness of the outcome continued to reflect how competitive Pennsylvania had become in presidential elections. The ABC Exit Poll revealed some interesting dynamics at work in the race. Women and men divided their votes in exactly opposite directions – women gave Dukakis 54 percent of their vote, and the men 46 percent, while Bush won 46 percent of the women and 54 percent of the men. Dukakis edged out Bush among Catholic voters 52 percent to 48 percent. Once again, as in the two previous presidential elections, the Republicans fared better among their voters than did the Democrats. Bush won 90 percent of his party's vote to Dukakis's 82 percent. African Americans, who gave Dukakis 91 percent of their votes, remained tremendously loyal to the Democrats.

Chapter 7
The Democrats Take Control: the 1990s

Few presidents have had such highs and lows as George H. W. Bush, whose job approval pushed 90 percent in the spring of 1991 in the wake of the stunning and quick victory over Saddam Hussein in the first Iraq war. Remarkably, less than two years later he earned only 38 percent of the vote in a failed bid for reelection. Bush's fall related directly to several domestic problems, the most important of which was a recession that struck in the summer of 1990. The economy worsened throughout the next year as retail spending declined, the real estate market slumped, and unemployment rose to seven percent. Bush divided his Republican base when he violated his own "no new taxes" pledge by reaching a compromise with congressional Democrats that led to increased taxes. Some conservatives, angry over the tax hikes and some other actions of the administration, rallied around Patrick J. Buchanan, a former Nixon speech writer, as an alternative.

Other early signs pointed to further political difficulty for the president. The Republicans lost a nationally watched special U.S. Senate election in 1991 to fill the term of Pennsylvania Senator John H. Heinz 3rd, who had been killed in a helicopter crash. The Republican candidate was Richard Thornburgh, Bush's former attorney general and former two-term Pennsylvania governor (1979-1987). Thornburgh lost to an opponent who had never sought elective office before and who was not considered a very effective campaigner, Harris Wofford. At the time of Heinz's death, Wofford was serving as Secretary of Labor and Industry in the administration of Governor Bob Casey, who appointed Wofford to replace Heinz. And though he had been an adviser to President Kennedy, Wofford was far from a household name when he faced Thornburgh in the election. In a campaign anticipating Bill Clinton's strategy in running for president in 1992, Wofford made the 1991 special election about the nation's economic distress, especially highlighting the cost and availability of health care. Two of the Wofford campaign managers who devised this strategy, James Carville and Paul Begala, were hired by Clinton to run his 1992 national campaign after their success in pulling off the stunning upset of Thornburgh in the Senate election.

1992: Bush and Clinton

Even though President Bush's popularity plummeted as 1992 approached, the Republican Party coalesced around him and prepared to send him back for another term. Bush did have a nominal opponent, Pat Buchanan. Although

Buchanan posed little practical electoral concern, he regularly reminded voters that Bush was not a genuine conservative, true to Reagan's conservative principles. Bush wrapped up the nomination by mid-March; his sweep in the "Super Tuesday" primaries effectively ended the nomination contest. Buchanan remained on the Pennsylvania ballot for the state's primary, but he was trounced 77 percent to 23 percent by the president, who won all the contested delegate votes.

Similar to the 1988 nomination battle, the Democrats had a crowded field of presidential candidates. Former Arkansas Governor Bill Clinton emerged as the early favorite among party leaders. Clinton was the quintessential rising star in the Democratic Party. Outgoing and charismatic, he was elected governor of his state in 1978; he was the youngest governor in the nation. Defeated in a reelection bid, he returned in 1982 and served four more terms. Clinton's programs in Arkansas focused on education and economic development. Nationally, he became a prominent member of the centrist Democratic Leadership Council.

During the primary season Clinton argued that he was a New Democrat, meaning he would crack down on crime, end welfare as currently practiced, and

President Bill Clinton works his way through the crowd at the Pittsburgh International Airport during a 1993 visit to the city. In the 1992 election, Clinton's success across Pennsylvania was the greatest for any Democrat since Lyndon Johnson's electoral victories in 1964. (Copyright, *Pittsburgh Post-Gazette*, 2006, all rights reserved. Reprinted with permission.)

ensure that all Americans had health care. Being a New Democrat also meant campaigning as a moderate, which proved popular with Democratic voters eager to win the presidency after twelve years of Republican control. He distanced himself from leftist rival Jesse Jackson, the civil rights leader, to demonstrate his moderation. Jackson had accepted contributions in past campaigns from Nation of Islam Minister Louis Farrakhan and had praised Cuban President Fidel Castro. At a conference sponsored by Jackson's Rainbow Coalition, Clinton castigated rapper Sister Souljah for her racist and provocative comments about whites. It was a dramatic moment, widely covered by the media.

Clinton ran into some stiff challenges in the opening delegate selection events, however. Senator Tom Harkin won his home state of Iowa. Then just prior to the New Hampshire primary, real trouble found Clinton. Throughout the campaign he was dogged by allegations of marital infidelity and draft-dodging. His answers were not always convincing, and doubts emerged as to whether he had the character to lead the nation. Clinton and his wife, Hillary, attempted to address public charges of marital infidelity in a celebrated appearance on CBS's *60 Minutes*. Hillary Clinton defended her husband, but doubts about his electability persisted. Despite these difficulties, Clinton wrapped up the nomination earlier than any Democrat in more than twenty years.

In the primaries, former Massachusetts Senator Paul E. Tsongas won New Hampshire, and Jerry Brown, former governor of California, won Colorado. March proved to be the critical month in the Democratic contest. Clinton clinched the nomination with a series of primaries on Super Tuesday, mostly in southern states. After Clinton's victories, his opponents' resources and support dried up. On April 7 Clinton won three big primaries in Minnesota, Wisconsin, and New York, but the latter with only 40 percent of the vote, leaving Pennsylvania's April 28 primary important but not decisive.

Still, Clinton did not take the Keystone State for granted. National polls during the spring showed him trailing President Bush in the 10-12 point range. Doubts about his electability still remained in late April; the state gave him an opportunity to assuage those doubts. After a week's rest in Arkansas, Clinton campaigned hard in Pennsylvania, traveling with Senator Harris Wofford. He took the unusual step of meeting with ward leaders in Philadelphia, and he received the coveted endorsement of an influential group of black ministers, the Black Clergy of Philadelphia. Finally, the unions, many of which earlier were not enthusiastic about Clinton, fell in line; Clinton secured the backing of the United Mine Workers and the United Steelworkers of America.

Clinton's only active opponent in the state was Jerry Brown, but faced with a united Democratic Party, Brown's prospects were dismal. Yet one powerful union in the state, the Service Employees International Union, angry with what they contended was Clinton's anti-union record as governor of Arkansas, endorsed

Brown. The Californian's whole strategy was to woo the labor vote in a state where unemployment was 7.3 percent, about the national average, but higher in some communities. He launched a full-fledged campaign in the state. In Erie he emphasized that the entire campaign was about who was working, insisting that "every person should be hired and given a job, and once you're hired, you should be paid enough to support your family." He addressed mostly small crowds, and his fate was largely sealed.[61]

Clinton romped to an easy 57 percent victory in the state, more than double Brown's 26 percent. It was, as expected, a low-turnout primary, which worried some Democratic leaders who feared that Clinton was not exciting voters with a tough general election ahead. Still, Clinton's victory provided some badly needed help on the character front – while only 50 percent of the voters in the New York primary several weeks before said that Clinton had the integrity and honesty to serve in the White House, Pennsylvania Democratic voters pushed the percentage above 60 percent.[62]

As the national convention in New York drew near, another potential problem developed for the Clinton campaign. This one involved the Democratic governor of Pennsylvania, Bob Casey, the subject of abortion, and a controversy that made national headlines. Typically, big-state governors are provided opportunities to speak at conventions, maybe not on primetime television, but at some point on the agenda. But Casey's request to give such an address was anything but simple. The governor's intended topic, abortion, was dynamite. Casey detested abortion on demand, as he called it, and he wanted to tell the convention attendees why. The governor's position put him at odds with the vast majority of the Democratic delegates and the position of Bill Clinton.

Casey had not endorsed Clinton, and he had long urged the Pennsylvania delegation to the national convention to remain neutral. Personally, he wanted a candidate without Clinton's moral shortcomings and, in ideological terms, an anti-abortion nominee. Otherwise, according to Casey, the general election was in doubt. The governor did not have his way, however. The state delegation overwhelmingly was committed to Clinton, consistent with the primary; 133 delegates were for Clinton, 50 for Jerry Brown, and only Casey and three other delegates were uncommitted.[63]

Earlier in Casey's gubernatorial tenure, the Pennsylvania legislature had passed and he had signed a bill placing restrictions on abortions in the state. The legislation led to a federal court appeal that ultimately became an important U.S. Supreme Court abortion precedent, upholding parts of Pennsylvania's law – namely, to require a 24-hour waiting period, informed consent (requiring doctors to notify a woman of the health risks involved), and parental consent for minors. Undeterred by the pro-choice sentiment at the New York convention, Casey believed many Democrats were likewise opposed to abortion and that they deserved a voice within the party. Furthermore he was riled that the Democratic Party, in his view, had been hijacked by pro-abortion rights activists, specifically by the National Abortion Rights Action League. Casey did not take the request to address the convention lightly, as he pointed out in his memoir, *Fighting for Life*. Months before the convention, Casey had appeared before the Democratic Platform Committee and made the same arguments about the diversity of abortion views within the party. He pointed out that in 1990 he had been reelected by more than one million votes over a pro-choice Republican opponent. He then appointed pro-choice Harris Wofford to assume Senator Heinz's seat and helped Wofford win election to complete Heinz's term in 1991. The appeal fell on deaf ears because the platform, when drafted, contained a strongly pro-choice position. Casey wrote to National Democratic Chairman Ron Brown with a request to address the convention, but he received no response. The ever-persistent Casey had a letter hand-delivered to the chairperson of the convention, and again no answer was forthcoming. Casey later found out that the parliamentarian of the convention had ruled his request out of order.[64]

In a show of dissatisfaction with Casey, the organizers of the convention relegated the Pennsylvania delegation to the rear of Madison Square Garden. But the governor did not give up the fight. On July 14, the day the convention adopted its abortion-rights plank, Casey arranged for a full-page advertisement to appear in the *New York Times* expressing misgivings about abortion and explicitly rejecting the notion that unelected Supreme Court justices had the authority to make abortion a constitutional right. The ad was signed by Democrats, Republicans, liberals, and conservatives, and included an impressive list of politicians, journalists, and academics.

Inside the convention hall, the drama continued. The convention's organizers invited a convention address by a pro-choice Republican woman from central Pennsylvania who had campaigned for Casey's 1990 opponent, Barbara Hafer. Stunned by the obvious insult, Casey refused to report the Pennsylvania vote, giving that honor to a state senator in the delegation. The governor sat out the presidential election. A year later he underwent a rare heart-and-liver transplant and turned over state government to his lieutenant governor, but he returned to his duties in time to set up an exploratory committee to wrest the party nomination from Clinton in 1996. He halted the effort in April 1996 because of recurring health problems.

Bob Casey may have been banished to the hinterlands of Madison Square Garden, but another Pennsylvania Democrat was on center stage. Ironically, the state's newest senator, Harris Wofford, who owed his appointment and much of his 1991 election to Casey, made it to Clinton's vice presidential short list as the convention drew near. In early July, David Martin, Washington correspondent for the *Harrisburg Patriot News*, reported that Wofford was among several members of

Congress under strong consideration. The list included Indiana Congressman Lee Hamilton and Clinton's ultimate choice, Senator Al Gore.[66]

The 1992 presidential election was further complicated by the emergence of a formidable third-party candidate, Ross Perot. Though personally eccentric, the Texas millionaire captured the discontent Americans felt for big government and the shaky economy; he staked his entire campaign on the rising federal deficit and a promise to balance the budget. Strangely, after leading the race nationally in early summer polls, he left the contest in July claiming that Republicans in Texas were planning to sabotage his daughter's wedding. Without warning and to the surprise of everyone, he reentered the race in October. With little chance of winning, he potentially could play the role of spoiler.

The Clinton campaign focused its attention on the economy, which was in slow recovery. Voters never accepted the fact that the recession of 1990-91 had ended. Furthermore, President Bush seemed unable to relate to average voters. His success in foreign matters seemed removed from the electorate by the fall of 1992, while Clinton's charm and charismatic personality allowed him to connect with voters.

Pennsylvania assumed a pivotal role in the fall campaign; no Democrat since 1948 had won the presidency without carrying Pennsylvania. At the outset of the campaign season, Clinton had a narrow lead in Pennsylvania, which he expanded as the campaign progressed. He led Bush by six points, 46 to 40 percent in the Pennsylvanian Poll in late March, and the margin increased by the fall to a 12-point edge in the Keystone Poll in October. Many voters believed he would do a better job of handling the most important issue of the campaign, the economy. Significantly, he led among most of the major demographic groups: men and women, Catholic and union households, African Americans and Jews. Among moderate voters, he held a commanding 17- point lead.

Additionally, Clinton's campaign operation in the state was better organized than the president's, with three full-time regional offices, eighty paid staff members, and 4,000 volunteers. Meanwhile, organizational problems racked Bush's Pennsylvania campaign. His campaign director left the state in mid-summer, and the campaign was late in developing a strategy to carry the state. Yet Bush made frequent visits to Pennsylvania, as did Clinton, many of them to the Philadelphia suburbs. Both campaigns were fully cognizant of the statewide political implications of winning the vote-rich suburbs.

Yet the election was not a landslide. In the end, it was a referendum on the incumbent, and the president lost. Nationally, Bush could only manage 38 percent of the popular vote, while Clinton won 43 percent. Perot did extraordinarily well, capturing 19 percent, which represented the votes of almost 20 million Americans. Clinton won the electoral vote decisively, 370 to Bush's 168. Perot's strong popular vote showing did not pay off with a single electoral vote.[66]

The Pennsylvania vote closely mirrored the national vote. Clinton earned almost a 500,000-vote victory, winning 45 percent over Bush with 36 percent and Perot with 18 percent. Perot did not carry a single county in the state. His best showing was in rural Elk County, where he received 28 percent; his worst result came in urban Philadelphia at 10 percent. Clinton's success at landing twenty-seven counties exceeded the total for any Democrat since Lyndon Johnson in 1964. His victory won back many of the constituencies lost during the last three presidential campaign cycles. He won the Reagan Democrats in the economically hard-hit, old industrial southwestern part of the state. He captured a higher share of the Philadelphia vote, 68 percent, than any Democrat since 1964, and he carried three of the four counties in the Philadelphia suburbs: Montgomery, Delaware, and Bucks. The loss of the suburbs by the Republicans was a harbinger of future losses in the voter-rich Philadelphia collar counties in subsequent presidential elections. Voter turnout in the state rose slightly from 1988; 55 percent of eligible voters cast ballots in 1992 compared to 52 percent in 1988.

The Pennsylvania Exit Poll, conducted for CNN, provided further context in which to understand the Clinton victory: he easily won female voters 48 percent to 35 percent for Bush; black voters 84 percent to eight percent for Bush; senior voters 52 percent to 37 percent for Bush. The Clinton campaign's focus on the economy and jobs paid dividends. Voters who believed their personal financial situations were worse than four years earlier overwhelming cast their votes for Clinton, 62 percent to 16 percent for Bush – and those voters constituted 42 percent of the election turnout. Those who believed they were better off, only 19 percent of the electorate, overwhelmingly voted for Bush, 64 percent to Clinton's 25 percent. Finally, among voters who said the economy was poor in 1992, 69 percent of them voted for Clinton while a paltry six percent cast votes for Bush. Even Ross Perot fared better than the president among voters still feeling the lingering effects of the recession. He won 22 percent of those who said the economy was poor. Voters who thought the economy was in good shape cast a large share of their votes for Bush. In the end, perceptions of the state of the economy upended Bush and brought Clinton to the White House.

The Democrats succeeded in halting a slide of three straight presidential elections in the state – though the narrowness of Clinton's victory set the stage for competitive races in the future. The state also maintained its position as one of the key battleground states.

1996: Clinton and Dole

Clinton's first presidential term was marked by two different stages of policies. In the first two years, he struggled with an unpopular administration plan to overhaul the nation's health care system and a debate over a proposal to allow gays in the military. As Clinton's standing with the American people eroded, the

Republicans captured both houses of Congress in the 1994 midterm elections. Realizing that his success as president depended on his ability to moderate his policies, he moved to the political center. There followed a welfare reform act that put more people previously on welfare into the work force, a tough crime-fighting law, and a balanced-budget approach that moved the nation toward more fiscal responsibility. A growing economy also assisted Clinton, whose approval rating rose to the 60 percent level in time for his reelection campaign in 1996.

The Republicans easily nominated Bob Dole, the majority leader of the Senate, a popular though somewhat dull campaigner who was available to run and seemed a safe choice. Dole was the consensus choice of Republicans, but Arlen Specter, Pennsylvania's senior U.S. senator, made a brief run at the Republican nomination – the first Pennsylvanian to seek the presidency since Governor Milton Shapp twenty years earlier. In Specter's autobiography, *Passion for Truth*, he describes the rationale for his candidacy. In 1994 and 1995 the senator reached the conclusion the nation was heading in the wrong direction, largely because of policies pursued by the Clinton White House and by legislators on Capitol Hill. In the case of Clinton, he objected to the president's health care plan, a massive 1,364-page piece of legislation that would have remade the health care system. Specter also complained that the president's Economic Recovery Act contained a large tax hike. In the case of Capitol Hill, he pointed out that he was the only Senate Republican to speak in favor of the 1994 crime bill. The final straw that motivated him into the race was Senator Bob Dole's opposition to an alternative health care plan developed by Specter and a handful of his Senate colleagues. Specter also believed, in his words, that only a "moderate" Republican could win the presidency against Clinton, and that a "right wing" effort was doomed.[67]

Specter began his campaign with exploratory travels on March 14, 1994, and he formally announced in front of the Lincoln Memorial on March 30, 1995. He opened offices in Des Moines, Iowa, and Manchester, New Hampshire. When Specter declared for the Republican nomination, it had the effect of freezing most Republican leaders in Pennsylvania from joining the campaigns of other candidates. The notable exception was the state's junior U.S. senator, Rick Santorum, who surprised many Republican leaders and especially his conservative supporters by endorsing Specter. What brought about the endorsement was immediately the subject of considerable discussion, mostly because of the differences in ideology and personalities between the two: Specter was moderate in ideology, analytical, and dispassionate by temperament, while Santorum was the darling of state's conservatives, outspoken, emotional, and at times fiery in demeanor.

With Santorum's rise to the Senate in 1995, he and Specter had worked out a *modus vivendi* for sharing their duties and daily activities in representing the state. This relationship, while practical, seemed surprising since Specter initially had adamantly opposed Santorum's candidacy for the Senate seat held most recently by Harris Wofford. Specter, determined to stop Santorum from running, actively tried to recruit another candidate. He approached David Eisenhower, the grandson of former President Dwight Eisenhower, and Theresa Heinz, the widow of Senator Heinz, but both refused to run. Then, surprisingly, after Santorum's nomination as the Republican candidate Specter supplied him with both financial resources and campaign staff, arguably making a big difference in helping him defeat Wofford. So, when Santorum endorsed Specter as a presidential candidate, it was viewed as returning a political favor. Even with Santorum's support, Specter never developed traction in the state. In April 1995, a Keystone Poll showed Specter trailing Bob Dole in Pennsylvania by 26 percentage points.

On the national campaign trail, Specter traveled frequently to the early convention delegate selection states, Iowa and New Hampshire, with side trips to other places. Specter's campaign literally went nowhere, in no small measure because of his pro-choice position on abortion. Both Iowa and New Hampshire were states in which social conservatives and pro-life activists dominated the Republican delegate-selection events. Other problems also developed. In June 1994 in Iowa, he was booed while delivering a speech dealing with the constitutional doctrine of church and state. Ultimately, party activists made it clear he would not be their choice; he ended his campaign abruptly on November 22, 1995.

Specter's withdrawal freed Republicans in Pennsylvania to proceed with their own presidential endorsements. Governor Tom Ridge endorsed Dole, which gave the Kansas senator access to the governor's organization and fundraising apparatus. Ridge's early support was undoubtedly a factor in placing him on Dole's short list of potential vice presidential running mates. No Pennsylvanian had been elected vice president since George Dallas served the Polk administration. However, one important factor in the selection is whether the nominee can deliver his home state. Had Ridge joined Dole on the ticket, their prospects in Pennsylvania would not have been enhanced. A July 1996 Keystone Poll provided the reason. More than half of the poll's respondents – 57 percent – indicated Ridge's addition to the Republican presidential ticket would make no difference in their vote, while equal numbers said it would make them either less likely or more likely to vote for the ticket – an identical 19 percent each. In any case, the Pennsylvania governor took himself out of the vice presidential sweepstakes before Dole made a selection. Pennsylvania voters seemed somewhat flattered by the attention Ridge received. Almost half of those polled, 46 percent, wanted Ridge to accept the nomination if offered – 53 percent of them were Republicans and 38 percent of them were Democrats. Dole ultimately selected former congressman and economic supply-sider Jack Kemp as his running mate.

In 1996, the voters of Pennsylvania had no practical role to play in the selection of the presidential nominees. Twenty-nine states preceded Pennsylvania in the process of picking convention delegates, including such delegate-rich states as New York, California, and Florida. Dole and Clinton had their respective nominations sewed up a month before Pennsylvania's April primary. Dole did campaign briefly in the state before the Republican primary, a mere two days in April. The Kansan had one remaining active national primary opponent in the race by the Pennsylvania primary, Patrick Buchanan, who chose to skip the state and campaign elsewhere. Other former Dole rivals technically remained on the ballot, but all of them had quit the race by mid-April. Similarly, Clinton campaigned minimally in the state prior to the primary. The Clinton strategy was to use television commercials, many of them paid for by party committees to keep the air waves filled with reminders of the Clinton agenda and to attack the Republicans for budget-cutting approaches that would reduce social safety-net programs.

Since the presidential primary was a minimal event, voter turnout in the state dropped to a mere 25 percent of the state's registered voters. The dismal showing compared unfavorably to the 40 percent turnout in the 1992 primary. Pennsylvania had, indeed, become irrelevant in the presidential selection process.

The fall campaign was not memorable. Dole promised a 15 percent tax cut, attempting to capture some of the lost Reagan luster. Clinton ran for reelection as the new centrist Clinton. Ross Perot entered the race again, this time as the candidate of his new Reform Party. Clinton had large leads in both national and Pennsylvania polls throughout the entire campaign. In late October, the Pennsylvania Keystone Poll provided a summary of the voters' thinking late in the campaign. Clinton had a 12-point lead a week before the election. The president led among his own core supporters, but his double-digit margin among key swing groups of moderates, independents, and Catholics ensured his ability to carry the state.

Still, the election was vigorously contested in the state. The Republicans did not give it away. In Villanova, Dole went after Clinton for what he called "the character of our country," an obvious reference to marital infidelities, and he accused the president of "liberal leniency," a reference to being soft on crime. Clinton reiterated the successes of his first term, and in Pennsylvania visits he pointed out the economic improvements made in the state during his presidency. In a big Philadelphia event in late September, he ate cheese steaks at Pat's, attended a $1,000-per-person cocktail fundraiser, and talked politics with everyday Philadelphians.[68]

The general election results were a foregone conclusion. Nationally, Clinton easily won reelection, but could not reach the 50 percent mark. The presence of Perot undoubtedly prevented the president from claiming a majority of the popular vote. He won 49 percent to Dole's 41 percent and Perot's eight percent. The electoral vote was conclusive, 379 for Clinton to 159 for Dole. The president's victory was accomplished by winning the votes of women in huge numbers;

he led Dole by 14 points, especially among single women, while also capturing moderate voters by 24 points, and independents by eight points. Clinton's victory can largely be explained by the general health of the economy and the absence of a divisive war. As his gain among moderate voters showed, he had successfully redefined himself as a centrist.

Clinton won Pennsylvania, but here also he was denied a majority of the popular vote, winning 49 percent to 40 percent, while Perot won 10 percent, slightly more than half of his share in 1992. Clinton won twenty-eight counties, one more than in 1992. Once again the president carried three of the four suburban counties in the southeastern part of the state, and by slightly larger majorities. His Philadelphia margin was ten percentage points higher in 1996 than four years earlier, but Dole cut into Clinton's base in the southwestern part of the state. The Voter News Service Exit Poll for Pennsylvania spelled out the particulars of Clinton's victory. The president narrowly defeated Dole among male voters, 46 to 42 percent, but his edge among women was decisive, 53 to 38 percent, as was his victory among African Americans, 90 to eight percent. The growing economy benefited the incumbent president. One-third of the voters said they believed their financial situation had improved over the preceding four years and Clinton won their votes, 62 to 32 percent over Dole, an increase of 37 points for Clinton from 1992.

Ross Perot was substantially less of a factor in the state in 1996 than he had been in 1992. His 10 percent of the vote was drawn almost evenly from Democrats and Republicans, and his absence from the race probably would not have changed the outcome. As a group, Perot's supporters were more pessimistic about economic recovery and viewed the future with more alarm. They were more likely than supporters of Clinton or Dole to believe the country was moving in the wrong direction, to cite the economy and jobs as the most important issue facing the country, and to indicate that life would be worse for the next generation of Americans.

The 1990s proved to be important rebuilding years for Pennsylvania Democrats. They stemmed the tide of three straight Republican presidential victories in the state. And even though Bill Clinton's state victories were achieved without winning a majority of the popular vote, he had made significant inroads into the Republican suburbs and made the four counties around Philadelphia the new battleground in the state. In the new century, the state would tilt towards the Democrats, but Pennsylvania would remain competitive in presidential elections.

Chapter 8
Elections in the New Century

The nation entered the new century evenly divided between the two major parties, which made battleground states such as Pennsylvania all the more pivotal in presidential elections. Democrats continued to win presidential elections in the Keystone state, though both the 2000 and 2004 elections were hotly contested and very close. The state continued to play no role in nominations, which were wrapped up before the April primary. But Pennsylvania had become one of twelve or fifteen states that were genuinely competitive in deciding the outcome of presidential elections. As a result of the closeness of the contests, candidates visited Pennsylvania frequently to raise money and hold public events.

2000: Bush and Gore

The Democrats had little doubt about nominating Vice President Al Gore. Gore had been a loyal Clinton ally, but the Clinton impeachment by the House for perjury and obstruction of justice related to his sexual relationship with a White House intern, Monica Lewinsky, forced Gore to walk a tightrope even narrower than the one usually facing vice presidents. He had to be his own man, but he needed the help and support of Clinton's loyal party activists and voters. He capitalized on the prosperity of the late 1990s. A federal surplus produced a national debate on how to spend the government's newfound billons. The nation enjoyed the lowest unemployment in more than twenty-five years; it dropped to 4.1 percent in 1991. Gore had his own ideas on using the surplus. He promised a new era of increased spending on popular government programs such as education, health care, and entitlement programs. The nation was also at peace. Despite attacks on American interests by Islamic terrorists, little public or media attention was paid to the growing threat from groups such as Al Qaeda, which had set up training camps in Afghanistan.

Gore's chief rival for the nomination was U.S. Senator Bill Bradley from New Jersey, a Princeton All-American, Rhodes Scholar, and New York Knicks basketball star. Bradley entered the race as a reformer, pledging to run a campaign based on "new ideas," notably questioning how Congress was spending the recently acquired federal surplus. At the same time, he targeted campaign finance reform and gun control. His campaign never gained support, however, among the core constituencies in the Democratic Party. Though he did have basketball superstar Michael Jordan campaigning for him in the early primaries, his failure to win in Iowa or New Hampshire sealed his fate, and he ended his campaign in early

March. He remained on the Pennsylvania ballot and won one-fifth of the Democratic primary vote without doing anything actively to achieve it.

The Republican nomination was essentially a two-person race between the moderate Texas Governor George W. Bush, son of President George H.W. Bush, and conservative Arizona Senator John McCain, a popular Vietnam War veteran who had been imprisoned and tortured during the war. Bush campaigned on his record as governor of Texas, as a unifier, and on the general theme of compassionate conservatism. McCain, similar to Bradley, entered the race as a reformer stressing many of the same themes as his New Jersey colleague. He wanted the federal government reformed systemically, federal campaign finances laws overhauled, and federal spending reduced. McCain did surprisingly well in the early primaries, skipping the Iowa caucus but thumping Bush by 19 points in New Hampshire. He then lost South Carolina in a bitter and divisive contest highlighted by phone calls to potential voters that suggested McCain had fathered an illegitimate black child. An embittered McCain continued, but by March 7, Bush had won nine states, McCain four, and on Super Tuesday Bush clinched the nomination. He won nine of the thirteen states in play. McCain ended his campaign in mid-March. The Pennsylvania primary produced no surprise. Bush won 72 percent of the vote, and McCain, though gone from the contest, remained on the ballot and chalked up 22 percent.

After Bush and Gore dispatched their opponents, little was left in the nomination contests except the lengthy drama of selecting running mates. For Pennsylvania Governor Tom Ridge, national speculation about his possible selection was in full swing by March and continued until mid-July of 2000. Bush himself confirmed that the governor was under serious consideration. Ridge filled out a vice presidential questionnaire and submitted it on June 22 to Dick Cheney, head of Bush's search team. The Pennsylvania governor certainly had strong credentials for the vice presidency. He also had a made-for-Hollywood resume. Born in Pittsburgh's Steel Valley, he was raised in a working-class family and grew up in veterans' housing. He won a scholarship to Harvard and after graduation entered Dickinson Law School. His legal studies were interrupted by the military draft. Ridge served in the army in Vietnam, where he was awarded several combat medals, including the Bronze Star. Ridge added to his credentials by serving as an assistant district attorney in Erie County, followed by election to Congress in 1982 and the governorship in 1994.

By 2000, Ridge had a record of substantial accomplishment as governor, a 60 percent approval rating, and he was the chief executive of a major large swing state. Ridge had been considered by Bob Dole in 1996 as a possible running mate and his easy reelection in 1998 only fueled interest in a bid for the presidency or vice presidency. When the governor undertook a series of national and international trips, raising his visibility, speculation ran rampant about national office.

Public opinion polls in the state showed that Ridge would help Bush carry the state in the general election, which was a reversal of what the Keystone Poll showed in 1996 when Ridge was under consideration by Bob Dole. A March Keystone Poll examined how a Bush-Ridge ticket might fare among Democrats in the state, especially among conservative Democrats. The findings demonstrated that the addition of Ridge would be somewhat helpful among social conservatives, especially those living in Pittsburgh and in the southwestern part of the state, among conservative born-again Christians, and among Democrats who opposed gun control.

But Ridge's nomination was not to be. He turned down an interview with Cheney in early July, but kept it private that he had withdrawn his name from consideration. Bush eventually chose Cheney, the former Reagan Defense Secretary and Wyoming congressman, to be his running mate.[69]

The Republican convention was held in Philadelphia in late July at the First Union Center (later the Wachovia Center), the sixth Republican convention to be held in the city since the first one in 1856. Little happened inside the convention that was not well scripted, with even the drama of the Cheney vice presidential selection concluded before the convention began. Outside the convention left-wing and fringe groups flooded into downtown streets and more than four hundred individuals were arrested, but amidst a big police presence the convention activities were uninterrupted. At the end of the convention, the Republican Party was unified behind the Bush-Cheney ticket.

As the campaign progressed, Bush ran against the scandals of the Clinton era and promised to restore trust in the presidency. His continued use of the expression "compassionate conservative" while on the campaign trail gained widespread currency. In policy terms, the expression meant that his administration would support increased social, education, and health expenditures, while also promising a middle-class tax cut.

Both candidates' strategies called for spending the lion's share of their campaign resources in the twelve to fifteen battleground states. As one of those states, Pennsylvania was important and hard-fought. The campaigns flooded the air waves with commercials, and the candidates and their surrogates visited the key states frequently. The visits began more than a year before the election, much earlier than in previous cycles, with the leading contenders trouping into the state to raise money. Bush, with enthusiastic assistance from Ridge, held four fundraisers in a two-day period in June 1999, raising one million dollars. The Pennsylvania governor's endorsement brought with it a plethora of advantages, including his impressive network of supporters and fundraisers. By early February 2000, Ridge had raised almost three million dollars for the Bush campaign. The Republican establishment moved fast and early to get on the Bush bandwagon. Twenty of the thirty Republican state senators signed onto the Bush campaign, as did two major statewide office holders and five members of Congress. On the Democratic side, the Gore people held a $1,000-per-plate fundraiser in June 1999 at the Franklin Plaza Hotel in Philadelphia. The event hosted by Mayor Ed Rendell raised $500,000.[70]

By early September 2000, the parties and interest groups in Pennsylvania had already spent five million dollars on television. The candidates and their surrogates campaigned furiously. The vice president made nineteen trips to the state, Governor Bush thirteen. Three of Gore's visits came in the last week, while the Democratic vice presidential candidate Joseph Lieberman, a Connecticut U.S. senator, traveled into the state twice. Bush and Cheney also visited three times during the last week of the campaign.[71]

Gore had a fairly sizable 13-point lead in the late September Keystone Poll – 49 to 36 percent. The Bush campaign waged a vigorous comeback and narrowed the gap to a one-point edge the week before the election – 43 percent to 42 percent, with one in ten voters undecided on the eve of the election. Voters in the state generally preferred Gore's positions on the issues while finding Bush more likable. The campaign settled into a debate over entitlement programs, Social Security, Medicare, and taxes, mostly issues that had tended to favor Democrats over Republicans in recent decades.

The national election returns showed a closely divided electorate. Gore won 51 million to Bush's 50.5 million votes. But Bush won the electoral vote, which was also close, 271 to 267 – one more than the 270 votes necessary for election. The election hinged on the state of Florida with its 25 electoral votes. The closeness of the election forced a series of recounts that ended with Bush declared the winner by Florida election officials. Democrats argued that many votes remained uncounted or were not counted properly. The Gore campaign contested the results in the courts, and in an historic 5-to-4 ruling the Supreme Court ended the manual recounts, giving Bush the 25 electoral votes and the election. This election polarized the nation and the bitterness over the disputed outcome carried into 2004 and beyond. Democrats believed that the will of the electorate had been thwarted by the judicial system, while Republicans felt that the Democrats had attempted to steal the election.

In Pennsylvania Gore prevailed with 51 percent to Bush's 47 percent. He won by 205,000 out of about 4.9 million votes. Ralph Nader, the consumer activist and nuclear power opponent on the Green Party ticket, was a non-factor in the race, winning only two percent of the vote. He had only polled at five percent in the Keystone Poll released a week before the election, and almost half of his supporters indicated they might alter their choice – something that was borne out in the final election returns. Turnout of eligible voters increased as 54 percent voted in 2000 compared to 50 percent who turned out in 1996.

Gore's victory in the state was similar in its geographic and ideological patterns to Bill Clinton's earlier victories, mirroring voting patterns of previous presidential elections. Still, Gore did something that had eluded Clinton in 1992 and 1996; he won a majority of the popular vote. The regional composition of the vote explained not just Gore's victory but also the changing nature of regional voting patterns. Leading the way for Gore was a huge 80 percent majority in Philadelphia – a 348,000-vote margin, the largest edge for any presidential candidate since Lyndon Johnson defeated Goldwater in 1964 by 430,000 votes. Gore won only eighteen counties, nine of them in the eastern part of the state and nine of them in the west, but nothing in the heartland of the state.

Crucial to his victory was his edge over Bush in the Philadelphia suburbs; he carried Bucks, Montgomery, and Delaware counties. His overall victory in the suburbs by 60,000 votes made it difficult for the Republicans to win the state. The vice president also won Allegheny County convincingly by almost 90,000 votes; this, combined with the vote in the southeast, Philadelphia and its four suburban counties, comprised almost 60 percent of Gore's total.

Bush could find some consolation in the southwestern part of the state, where he did better than the Republican presidential hopefuls in the previous three presidential elections. Voters there remained more culturally conservative than many of the Democratic candidates, and Reagan's presidency exercised a pull toward more conservative candidates while liberal Democratic candidates increasingly repelled them. By the new century, the slow realignment of voters in the old manufacturing counties of the southwest – Beaver, Westmoreland, Washington, Cambria, and Fayette – was taking its toll on Democratic candidates. Voters in the region cast their ballots for Democrats in most instances, but by margins substantially less than their party registration. By 2000, the Democrats, more than ever, came to rely on the vote of the big cities, which became a larger percentage of the party's vote. Republicans came to rely on the rural voters of the state's heartland along with the non-Philadelphia suburban voters. Philadelphia suburbanites became the key swing voters.

Undoubtedly Gore carried Pennsylvania because of how well he did among key demographic groups. According to the Voter News Service Pennsylvania 2000 Exit Poll, he won women, 58 percent to 40 percent, blacks by an amazing 90 percent, seniors (65 and older) by 60 percent to 38 percent, and union households 65 percent to 32 percent. Among the three swing voting groups, Gore narrowly won independents, 48 percent to 45 percent, and Catholics, 50 percent to 45 percent, but he earned a sizable margin among self-described moderate voters, 59 percent to 39 percent. Bush maintained a competitive edge by defeating Gore among men, 54 percent to 43 percent; married voters, 53 percent to 45 percent; and Protestants, 55 to 43 percent.

At the conclusion of the 2000 election, Pennsylvania was among the top ten most competitive states, and among the most competitive, only Florida had more electoral votes.

2004: Bush and Kerry

The 2004 election was set against the backdrop of the September 11, 2001, attacks on the United States and the global war on terror. In response, President Bush took the country to war in Afghanistan and Iraq. With the election set in the context of war, national security was seen by voters as the most important issue and the president capitalized on his strength as a war-time president. He rallied the nation by referring to the enemy as the "axis of evil," reminiscent of Ronald Reagan's characterization of the Soviet Union as the "evil empire."

During the first two years of his term Bush governed as a conservative, securing tax cuts, arguing for faith-based initiatives, and pushing his "No Child Left Behind" legislation for tougher school accountability through Congress. He also actively engaged in the 2002 midterm election, and he was substantially responsible for the Republicans increasing their majorities in both houses of Congress, the first time Republicans had done so since 1924. Bush had no opponent in his drive toward a second term.

For the Democrats, the closeness of the 2000 election, the unpopularity of the Iraq war, and the increased polarization between Democratic and Republican party leaders generated a large field of ten mostly experienced candidates running for the nomination. But surprisingly Al Gore was not among them, despite the fact that he had won the popular vote four years earlier. Democrats had a weak economy going for them, as well as a high level of intensity among their core voters because of the contested 2000 election. They were spoiling for a rematch. They also had history on their side. No president had ever lost the popular vote and won reelection.

Of the field, Governor Howard Dean of Vermont made the strongest showing in the early stages of the campaign. He opposed the Iraq War and, unlike the other frontline candidates, ran against the Washington establishment. Dean attracted a group of young activists and made effective use of the Internet for communication and fundraising. He also won a December 2003 endorsement from Al Gore. His most serious opponents were two senators: John F. Kerry of Massachusetts and John Edwards of North Carolina. Kerry's most impressive credentials were his military service in Vietnam and his experience in the Senate. Both proved to be mixed blessings, the war service because of controversies over his battlefield decorations, and his Senate career because of a liberal voting record. Edwards was still in his first Senate term, and he lacked the experience of the other candidates; yet he was articulate and a southerner, the latter a considerable advantage since the three Democrats elected to the presidency beginning in 1964 had been southerners.

Kerry jumped out fast in the delegate selection hunt. He won the Iowa caucus and the New Hampshire primary. Following a loss in Iowa, the Dean campaign disintegrated after a horrific evening appearance by the candidate. In what

During his reelection campaign in the summer of 2004, President George W. Bush, surrounded by wary Secret Service agents, exits a limousine to greet a waiting crowd at the Safe Harbor Dam on the Susquehanna River southwest of Lancaster. (Photograph by Richard Hertzler, Lancaster *New Era*)

has been called the "I Have a Scream" speech, Dean let out a spontaneous holler that made him appear to have lost emotional control. The media coverage of the event was relentless, and the Dean campaign never recovered. Kerry then proceeded to win five of the seven primaries on "Junior Tuesday," February 3, while Edwards captured his neighboring state, South Carolina. Then on March 9, Super Tuesday, Kerry wrapped up the nomination; he captured nine of the ten primaries on that day, the earliest in a contested nomination in history. Kerry now had almost four months to continue to campaign before his party's Boston convention, to raise money, and to build a national organization for the general election. Similarly, President Bush secured enough delegate votes to win renomination by Super Tuesday. Without an opponent, he had the luxury of being able to attack Kerry immediately after clinching the nomination. The Democratic convention in Boston in late July was largely a love-fest. The party was united and a major effort was made to present Kerry's Vietnam War background as a major qualification for his election.

Within twenty-four hours of the convention's adjournment, Kerry was in Pennsylvania campaigning with his vice presidential running mate, John Edwards. From Scranton to Harrisburg and then to other places in the state, Kerry made it clear that the state was essential to a presidential victory. Most analysts concurred, believing that Kerry could not win the presidency without the state's twenty-one electoral votes.

The Republican convention was held in late August in New York City amidst heavy security against the backdrop of the ruined World Trade Center, the site of the 9/11 attack. The Republicans hoped to generate enthusiasm among the nation's voters by instilling a sense of patriotism in the campaign. President Bush's master campaign strategist, Karl Rove, appeared before the Pennsylvania delegation and laid out the Bush turnout strategy for reelection. According to Rove, because it was going to be difficult to win the traditional Republican suburbs, he had developed a voter-turnout plan he called the "exurb" strategy. Exurbs were outlying areas beyond the old suburbs, where people had moved in search of less crowded conditions, lower-cost housing, and good schools. South central Pennsylvania was a quintessential exurb, and the Bush strategy lay in increasing the turnout of core Republican voters there. Particularly important were social conservatives, who would offset the loss of moderate Republicans in the suburbs and the expected large percentage of votes the Democrats would win in the big cities.

Going into the Republican convention, the race nationally was very close. The Republicans gained a larger than usual "bounce" after almost a week of attention paid to national security and attacks on Kerry's record. As Labor Day passed, Bush opened up a five- to seven-point lead in the national polls.

In Pennsylvania as well, the contest remained competitive throughout the fall campaign. The Keystone Poll indicated that among likely voters Kerry held a six-point lead, 49 to 43 percent in late September. By late October the race was still very close, with Kerry holding a five-point lead, 51 to 46 percent. The Kerry lead just prior to the election was the first time either of the candidates emerged with a majority of the popular vote, another indicator of the competitiveness of the race in the state. In fact, beginning with the first of six Keystone polls, the lead bounced back and forth several times.

The Keystone Poll also identified the major issues the voters of the state thought important as they prepared to vote: terrorism and homeland security, both of which favored Bush's electoral chances. Voters who believed the nation was safer in 2004 said they would vote for Bush, and those who felt less safe were more likely to vote for Kerry. Kerry was helped also by those voters who thought the Iraq War was the most important issue. He was further aided by the president's weak job performance rating. Forty-six percent believed he was doing an excellent or good job, while 56 percent said he was doing only a fair or poor job in office. The low job performance related to nagging concerns about the economy, the rising costs of health care, and a perception that the president's domestic agenda, notably his tax cuts, favored the wealthy.

In the final days of the campaign, the national media and the candidates focused on the crucial swing states, Florida, Ohio, and Pennsylvania. Pennsylvania was the most-visited state during the election season. From President Bush's inauguration in January 2001 until election day in 2004, he visited the state forty-four times, the majority of them connected to his reelection. Kerry, who lived part of the time in the Pittsburgh suburbs, campaigned in the state more than twenty times. His home in the state was owned by his wife, Teresa Heinz Kerry, the widow of U.S. Senator John Heinz. She was a popular figure, especially in the western part of the state where her charitable and foundation work made her a genuine asset to Kerry.

As expected, the election results turned out to be very similar to 2000. The electoral pattern was almost identical. Only three states changed their votes; Iowa and New Mexico switched from Gore in 2000 to Bush in 2004, and Kerry won New Hampshire, which Bush had previously carried. Voter turnout increased to 122 million or 61 percent, 17 million more than in 2000. Bush won the popular vote decisively by 3 million votes or 51 percent. The closeness of the electoral vote once again caused the election results to be questioned, especially in Ohio, where a shift of 60,000 votes would have created another Florida-style election crisis. The president won 286 electoral votes to Senator Kerry's 252, or 16 more than the necessary majority. Florida and Ohio, two electoral-rich, pivotal states, went Republican, which assured Bush of the election. Pennsylvania went Democratic as it had in 2000.

Bush lost Pennsylvania, 48 percent to 51 percent, but by fewer votes than he did against Gore. He lost by only 144,000 out of almost 5.7 million votes cast. The Democrats captured only thirteen counties, but the Democratic percentage in them, especially in the two big cities and the Philadelphia suburbs, made the difference. The 96,000-vote edge in Allegheny County was 57 percent of the vote, and when added to a sizable 412,000 margin or 80 percent of the vote in Philadelphia gave Kerry 508,000 of his 2.9 million votes in the state. He carried three of the four Philadelphia suburban counties, Delaware, Montgomery, and

Bucks, by slightly more than 97,000 votes, and he lost heavily Republican Chester County by just 10,000 votes. Bush did better in the state than he did in 2000 because he did better in the southwest and northeast and held his own in the Republican central portion of the state. But still the Rove "exurb" strategy did not produce enough votes in the counties adjacent to the suburbs to carry the state for Bush. To win, Bush needed to do better in the Republican regions, especially the southeast. His increased vote totals made the state close. In fact, Pennsylvania turned out to be the sixth-most competitive state in the 2004 election.[72]

The Pennsylvania Exit Poll, conducted by the National Election Pool, indicated the president improved his vote totals among women by six points over 2000, losing to Kerry more narrowly 54 percent to 46 percent, but he defeated Kerry among men as he did in 2000, eking out a 51 percent to 48 percent victory. Bush picked up nine points among black voters, losing to Kerry 84 percent to 16 percent, keeping the senator well below the 90 percent mark. Republicans increased the share of their own partisans by seven percentage points from 2000, winning 89 percent, showing the success of the Rove strategy. Kerry won 85 percent of Democrats, about the same as Gore had four years earlier. But it was among independents that Kerry's margin proved decisive. Comprising 20 percent of the vote, independents went 58 percent to 41 percent for Kerry, a four-point decline from 2000 though still sufficient to be a significant factor in the outcome of the Pennsylvania race. As expected, the liberal Kerry won 88 percent of the liberal vote and the conservative president won 86 percent of conservatives. The crucial moderate vote, 30 percent of the total voters, was carried by Kerry 57 percent to 43 percent.

The votes of Catholics, 35 percent of the total voters in the state, were won by Kerry, but just barely, 51 percent to 49 percent. In recent years more attention has been paid to church attendance as a factor in voters' choices between Democratic and Republican candidates. In Pennsylvania, for example, Bush soundly defeated Kerry among people attending church more than once a week, 62 percent to 38 percent, and among once-a-week attendees, 55 percent to 45 percent. Those who did not attend church at all favored Kerry 68 percent to 31 percent, and those who attended a few times a year favored him 56 percent to 43 percent.

Four issues mattered most to Pennsylvania voters: terrorism, the Iraq war, moral values, and the economy. Bush easily won the support of the voters who cited terrorism, 83 percent to 17 percent, and moral values, 80 to 19 percent. Kerry by far carried the voters who said the Iraq war mattered most to them (71 percent over 29 percent for Bush) and those who cited the economy (82 percent for Kerry over 18 percent for Bush). In this battleground state, the issues divided voters by wide margins even as election results remained close.

Conclusion

Since 1932 Pennsylvania politics has gone through an enormous transition from a one-party state to one of the most competitive states in the nation. The New Deal realignment began the process of establishing genuine two-party competition, and Philadelphia's conversion to the Democrats in the 1950s completed the transition. The first demonstration of the new competitiveness occurred in the razor-tight 1960 contest won by John F. Kennedy. It was also the first year in which the Democrats obtained a voter registration majority. Thereafter, though once neglected in national politics as a quintessential Republican state, Pennsylvania moved into the center of presidential politics.

Pennsylvania has shown a tendency to pick winners. In the twelve presidential elections that followed 1960, the state's votes were cast for the winning presidential candidate nine times. The state went for losing candidates only with Hubert Humphrey in 1968, Al Gore in 2000, and John Kerry in 2004 (and Gore was the national popular vote victor). Although important in the voting, Pennsylvania seldom fielded candidates of its own. Pennsylvania has sent only one president to the White House, James Buchanan back in 1856. Though favorite sons have been put forward largely to maintain control over the convention delegations, Bill Scranton in 1964 was the only Pennsylvanian in more recent times to gain national attention and even a remote prospect for success.

Despite its competitiveness and its emergence as a swing state in general elections, after 1968 Pennsylvania became largely a non-factor in the presidential nomination process. As states moved their delegate selection events forward in the election calendar and as more states adopted primaries to choose delegates, Pennsylvania became irrelevant in the nomination of presidential candidates.

But in 2008, for the first time since 1984, Pennsylvania Democratic voters participated in a vigorously waged presidential primary contest. Senators Hillary Clinton and Barack Obama fought to a near-draw in the front-loaded primaries and caucuses between early January and March 4. For Pennsylvania, this resulted in reversing more than two decades of meaningless primaries. The state's Democratic voters gained a relevant seven-week primary campaign and the opportunity to cast a preference vote and select delegates in an election in which the Democratic nominee was not yet decided. Ironically, the state gained its relevance because the Pennsylvania legislature refused to move the primary forward in the election calendar.

In general elections, Pennsylvania remained a battleground. Beginning in the 1980s, the competitiveness became even more pronounced. The largest percentage earned by any presidential candidate from 1980 through 2004 was the 53 percent won by Republican Ronald Reagan in 1984. Then during the 1990s and into the new century, Pennsylvania tilted more toward the Democrats. The Democrats won the state in each of the four presidential elections between 1992 and 2004, but the margins of victory were small, leaving the state up for grabs.

Democrats have held a slight edge because they increased their percentage of the vote in Philadelphia and Pittsburgh, and beginning in 1992 they captured the suburbs in the southeast region and in the Lehigh Valley – areas with a large share of registered Republican voters. Overall, the voters in the state have tended in these elections to vote for moderate candidates. Since 1960, large portions of the electorate in the state have shown a willingness to evaluate candidates irrespective of party, and ticket splitting has become quite prevalent, especially in the southwestern part of the state, the Lehigh valley, and the Philadelphia suburbs.

Pennsylvania Presidential Elections, 1932-2004
By Party

Year	Total Vote	Winner	Pct (R)	Pct (D)	Pct Other
1932	2,859,177	R	50.84	45.33	3.83
1936	4,138,436	D	40.84	56.88	2.28
1940	4,078,714	D	46.33	53.23	0.44
1944	3,794,793	D	48.36	51.14	0.51
1948	3,735,348	R	50.92	46.91	2.16
1952	4,580,969	R	52.74	46.85	0.41
1956	4,576,503	R	56.49	43.30	0.21
1960	5,006,541	D	48.74	51.06	0.21
1964	4,822,690	D	34.70	64.92	0.37
1968	4,747,928	D	44.02	47.59	8.39[1]
1972	4,592,105	R	59.11	39.13	1.76
1976	4,620,787	D	47.73	50.40	1.87
1980	4,561,501	R	49.59	42.48	7.94[2]
1984	4,844,903	R	53.34	45.99	0.67
1988	4,536,251	R	50.70	48.39	0.91
1992	4,959,810	D	36.13	45.15	18.73[3]
1996	4,495,524	D	40.07	49.29	10.78[4]
2000	4,912,185	D	46.44	50.61	2.95
2004	5,765,764	D	48.46	50.96	0.59

[1] Percentage includes the American Independent Party candidate, George Wallace, who won 7.97% of the vote.
[2] Percentage includes the Independent candidate, John Anderson, who won 6.42% of the vote.
[3] Percentage includes the Independent candidate, Ross Perot, who won 18.20% of the vote.
[4] Percentage includes the Reform Party candidate, Ross Perot, who won 9.59% of the vote.

Source: http://staffweb.wilkes.edu/harold.cox/pres/indexpres.html

Notes

1. See Joe William Trotter's *River Jordan, African American Urban Life in the Ohio Valley* (Lexington, Ky.: University of Kentucky Press, 1998), for an important account of the changing status of blacks in the period; Andrew Buni, *Robert L. Vann of the Pittsburgh Courier: Politics and Black Journalism* (Pittsburgh: University of Pittsburgh Press, 1974),193-94.

2. H. F. Alderfer and Robert M. Sigmond, *Presidential Elections by Pennsylvania Counties 1920-1940* (State College, Pa.: Pennsylvania State College, 1941), 61; Richard C. Keller, *Pennsylvania's Little New Deal* (New York: Garland Publishing Inc., 1982), contains an excellent analysis of the politics of the New Deal in Pennsylvania.

3. Herbert Eaton, *Presidential Timber* (New York: Free Press of Glencoe, 1967), 321-360; Joseph F. Guffey, *Seventy Years on the Red-Fire Wagon* (Privately Printed, 1952), 172.

4. Michael Weber, *Don't Call Me Boss: David Lawrence, Pittsburgh's Renaissance Mayor* (Pittsburgh: University Press of Pittsburgh, 1988), 52-54; Bruce M. Stave, *The New Deal and the Last Hurrah, Pittsburgh Machine Politics* (Pittsburgh: University Press of Pittsburgh, 1970), 32-33.

5. *New York Times*, July 10, October 31, November 7 and 9, 1932.

6. *Philadelphia Inquirer*, November 2, 1932.

7. Eaton, *Presidential Timber*, 361-65.

8. Keller's *Pennsylvania's Little New Deal* is an outstanding source for the state's politics of the 1930s.

9. John Rossi, "Philadelphia's Forgotten Mayor: S. Davis Wilson," *Pennsylvania History* 51 (April 1984): 154-165.

10. *Philadelphia Inquirer*, October 1, 1936.

11. Keller, *Pennsylvania's Little New Deal*, 239-241.

12. "Pennsylvania after the New Deal," *The New Republic*, May 6, 1940, 599-601.

13. John M. McLarnon, *Ruling Suburbia: John J. McClure and the Republican Machine in Delaware County, Pennsylvania* (Dover: University of Delaware Press, 2003), 132-133.

14. Eaton, *Presidential Timber*, 368-92; Hugh Scott, *Come to the Party* (Englewood Cliffs., N.J.: Prentice-Hall, 1968), 12-16; Dan Rottenberg, "The Sun Gods," *Philadelphia Magazine*, September 1975, 1-18.

15. *Guffey*, Seventy Years, 115-17, 126-27.

16. Weber, *Don't Call Me Boss*, 183.

17. Stephen B. Grove, "The Decline of the Republican Machine in Philadelphia, 1936-52" (Phd diss., University of Pennsylvania, 1976), 246-61.

18. Eaton, *Presidential Timber*, 402-9; Weber, *Don't Call Me Boss*,183-87.

19. Grove, "Decline of the Republican Machine," 392-93.

20. Frank Freidel, *Franklin D. Roosevelt: A Rendezvous with Destiny* (Boston: Little Brown and Company, 1990), 565.

21. Edward Martin's autobiography, *Always Be on Time* (Harrisburg: The Telegraph Press, 1958), is a useful account of Martin's political activities; Eaton, *Presidential Timber*, 410-25.

22. James A. Kehl, "Philadelphia, 1948: City of Crucial Conventions," *Pennsylvania History* 67 (Spring 2000): 313-26.

23. Weber, *Don't Call Me Boss*, 332.

24. William J. McKenna, "The Negro Vote in Philadelphia Elections," *Pennsylvania History*

32 (October 1965): 406-15.

25. Eaton, *Presidential Timber*, 454-82; Joseph S. Clark Papers, Box 22C, Historical Society of Pennsylvania.

26. "The President Maker," *Time*, June 30, 1952, 18-21; *New York Times*, November 11, 1951.

27. Eaton, *Presidential Timber*, 432-53.

28. Paul B. Beers, *Pennsylvania Politics Today and Yesterday: The Tolerable Accommodation* (University Park: The Pennsylvania State University Press, 1980), 179-85.

29. James A. Finnegan to Joseph S. Clark, June 9, 1956, Clark Papers, Box 26A, Historical Society of Pennsylvania.

30. Eaton, *Presidential Timber*, 483-88.

31. Jack M. Treadway, *Elections in Pennsylvania: A Century of Partisan Conflict in the Keystone State* (University Park: The Pennsylvania State University Press, 2005), 24-49.

32. Eaton, *Presidential Timber*, 507-10.

33. Eaton, *Presidential Timber*, 491-506.

34. Weber, *Don't Call Me Boss*, 359-65.

35. James Michener, *Report of the County Chairman* (New York: Random House, 1961), contains a full description of Michener's political activities.

36. Theodore H. White, *The Making of the President 1960* (New York: Atheneum Publishers, 1960), 326-33.

37. William J. McKenna, "The Influence of Religion in the Pennsylvania Elections of 1958 and 1960," *Pennsylvania History* 29 (October 1962): 407-19; Neal R. Peirce, *The Megastates of America* (New York: W.W. Norton & Company, 1972), 62-71.

38. John J. Kennedy, *Pennsylvania Elections: Statewide Contests from 1950-2004* (Lanham: University Press of America Inc., 2006), 175-76.

39. George D. Wolf, *William Warren Scranton—Pennsylvania Statesman* (University Park: The Pennsylvania State University Press, 1981), 53-55; McLarnon, *Ruling Suburbia*, 208-9.

40. Robert D. Novak's *The Agony of the G.O.P. 1964* (New York: The Macmillan Company, 1964) contains an excellent summary of Scranton's 1964 presidential effort. An exhaustive account of Scranton's presidential bid can be found in Wolf, *William Warren Scranton*, 86-121.

41. Beers, *Pennsylvania Politics*, 295-306.

42. Beers, *Pennsylvania Politics*, 295-306; Scott, *Come to the Party*, has an account of the Scranton 1964 nomination campaign.

43. Kennedy, *Pennsylvania Elections*, 176-77.

44. Lewis Chester, Godfrey Hodgson, and Bruce Page, *An American Melodrama, the Presidential Campaign of 1968* (New York: Viking, 1969), 153-54.

45. Beers, *Pennsylvania Politics,*184.

46. "Lurching Off to a Shaky Start," *Time*, September 20, 1968, http://www.time.com/time/printout/0,8816,838728,00.html.

47. Chester, *America Melodrama*, 624-25.

48. Kennedy, *Pennsylvania Elections*, 176-78.

49. S. A. Paolantonio, *Frank Rizzo: The Last Big Man in Big City America* (Philadelphia: Camino Books Inc., 1993), 145-47.

50. "The Confrontation of the Two Americas," *Time*, October 2, 1972,

http://www.time.com/time/printout/0,8816,906439,00.html.

51. Philip S. Klein and Ari Hoogenboom, *History of Pennsylvania* (University Park: The Pennsylvania State University Press, 1980), 529-31; Beers, *Pennsylvania Politics*, 363-409.

52. Beers, *Pennsylvania Politics*, 433-38.

53. Wolf, *William Warren Scranton*, 165-68.

54. Kennedy, *Pennsylvania Elections*, 179-81.

55. "The Day of the Underdogs," *Time*, May 5, 1980, http://www.time.com/time/printout/0,8816948845,00.html.

56. "The Mood of the Voter," *Time*, September 15, 1980. http://www.time.com/time/printout/0,8816,924432,00.html

57. "Clear Path to Re-nomination Presages Reagan Election Win," *Congressional Quarterly*, February 4, 1984, 221-24.

58. *Philadelphia Inquirer*, April 9, 1984.

59. These aspects of the campaign are covered by Jules Witcover in his *Party of the People: The History of the Democrats* (New York: Random House, 2003).

60. *The Pocono Record*, August 14, 1988.

61. *Philadelphia Inquirer*, April 16, 1992.

62. "Pennsylvania Primary Signals Breakthrough for Clinton," *Congressional Quarterly*, May 2, 1992, 1185.

63. *Wilkes-Barre Times Leader*, July 3, 1992.

64. *Reading Times*, July 13, 1992; Robert P. Casey, *Fighting for Life: Gov. Robert P. Casey* (Dallas: Word Publishing, 1996).

65. *Harrisburg Patriot-News*, July 10, 1992.

66. *Pittsburgh Post-Gazette*, October 16, 1992.

67. Arlen Specter with Charles Robbins, *Passion for Truth: from Finding JFK's Single Bullet to Questioning Anita Hill to Impeaching Clinton* (New York: Harper Collins Inc., 2000).

68. *Philadelphia Inquirer*, September 17, 25, 26, 1996.

69. *Erie Times-Leader*, March 5, 2000; *Philadelphia Inquirer*, July 26, 2000.

70. *Philadelphia Inquirer*, June 24, 1999.

7i. *New York Times*, September 10, 2000.

72. Kennedy, *Pennsylvania Elections*, 189-90.

Suggestions for Further Reading

Pennsylvania has a treasure trove of historical resources available to scholars. Many were useful in preparing this monograph and are listed in the bibliography. Others are worth recommending to readers seeking to learn more about Pennsylvania's history in presidential politics.

Some of the state's major political leaders have written memoirs or autobiographies that provide keen insights as well as rationalizations for their actions and decisions: Governors Edward Martin, Dick Thornburgh, and Robert Casey; and U.S. Senators Joseph Guffey, Edward Martin, Hugh Scott, and Arlen Specter.

Two excellent recent books dealing in part with Pennsylvania presidential elections and voter behavior are John J. Kennedy's *Pennsylvania Elections* and Jack M. Treadway's *Elections in Pennsylvania*; they were of special assistance in analyzing the implications of Pennsylvania presidential election trends and voter returns.

The standard text *Pennsylvania History* by Philip S. Klein and Ari Hoogenboom has a solid grasp of Pennsylvania politics and summarizes political and economic events and trends with accuracy. Paul Beers' *Pennsylvania Politics* contains a wealth of information and his vignettes dealing with the political personalities and political decision-making place his book on the indispensable list.

The state's newspapers were invaluable for their coverage of presidential campaigns especially the *Philadelphia Inquirer, Pittsburgh Post- Gazette, Harrisburg Patriot News, Scranton Times, Pocono Record, Reading Times, Wilkes-Barre Times Leader,* and the *Allentown Morning Call.*

Coverage of the election process and national nominating conventions since the 1960s has been comprehensive and entertaining. Before 1960, the best work available on the machinations of the nomination process and the details of convention activities is Herbert Eaton's *Presidential Timber*, which was extensively used for general background and convention analysis. Since then a spate of books has appeared. Theodore White has written four books covering presidential elections, *The Making of the President* for 1960, 1964, 1968, and 1972 – all are informative and entertaining if a bit romantic in their coverage.

For more than fifty years, *Congressional Quarterly* has provided extensive coverage of presidential elections. One can find in its weekly updates detailed information on the various primaries and caucuses leading up to the conventions complete with election returns and delegate counts. These were especially helpful in tabulating and analyzing the Pennsylvania primary returns.

National news magazines also have provided important coverage of

Pennsylvania political leaders and their roles in presidential campaigns. Especially informative were *Time*, *The Saturday Evening Post*, *Newsweek*, and *The New Republic*.

Statewide and/or county elections return data are available from many sources, including the *Pennsylvania Manual* published by the Commonwealth of Pennsylvania; in the previously mentioned books by John J. Kennedy and Jack M. Treadway; and on two websites, one maintained at Franklin & Marshall College, http://politics.fandm.edu, and at Wilkes University created by Harold Cox, http://staffweb.wilkes.edu/harold.cox/pres/indexpres/html.

For polling data before the 1980s, this work relied mostly on polls completed by the Gallup organization and reported in newspapers and news magazines. The *Pittsburgh Post-Gazette* sponsored the Pennsylvania Poll in the 1980s and the Keystone Poll, now produced at Franklin & Marshall College, began its work with the 1992 presidential election. The national television networks in recent years have used exit polls to assist in their post-election coverage. Over the years, they have employed a consortium of survey researchers. These polls have state components, and Pennsylvania's exit polls have been made available recently on the national network web sites.

Additional sources and further elaboration may be found on the website of the Pennsylvania History Studies Series: http://www.pa-history.org/pastudyseries.htm.

Bibliography

Beers, Paul B. *Pennsylvania Politics Today and Yesterday: The Tolerable Accommodation.* University Park: The Pennsylvania State University Press, 1980.

Boyer, Paul S., Clifford E. Clark Jr., Sandra McNair Hawley, Joseph F. Kett, Neal Salisbury, Harvard Sitkoff, and Nancy Woloch. *The Enduring Vision: A History of the American People.* Concise Third Edition. Boston: Houghton Mifflin Company, 1996.

Buni, Andrew. *Robert L. Vann of the Pittsburgh Courier: Politics and Black Journalism.* Pittsburgh: University of Pittsburgh Press, 1974.

Burnham, Walter Dean. *Critical Elections and the Mainsprings of American Politics.* New York: W.W. Norton & Company, 1970.

Carocci, Vincent P. *A Capitol Journey.* University Park: The Pennsylvania State University Press, 2005.

Casey, Robert P. *Fighting for Life: Gov. Robert P. Casey.* Dallas: Word Publishing, 1996.

Chester, Lewis, Godfrey Hodgson, and Bruce Page. *An American Melodrama, the Presidential Campaign of 1968.* New York: Viking Press, 1969.

Coben, Stanley. *A. Mitchell Palmer: Politician.* New York: Columbia University Press, 1963.

Cook, Rhodes. *The Presidential Nominating Process: A Place for Us?* New York: Rowan & Littlefield Publishers, Inc., 2004.

Cooke, Edward, and Edward Janosik. *Guide to Pennsylvania Politics.* New York: Greenwood Press, 1957.

Cooke, Edward. "Patterns of Voting in Pennsylvania Counties, 1944-1958." *Pennsylvania History* 27 (January 1960): 69-87.

David, Paul T., Ralph Goldman, Richard C. Bain. *The Politics of National Party Conventions.* Menasha: The Brookings Institution, 1960.

Eaton, Herb. *Presidential Timber.* New York: Free Press of Glencoe, 1967.

Ershkowitz, Miriam, and Joseph Zikmundi II, eds. *Black Politics in Philadelphia.* New York: Basil Books, 1973.

Fausold, Martin L. *Gifford Pinchot: Bull Moose Progressive.* Syracuse: Syracuse University Press, 1961.

Freidel, Frank. *Franklin D. Roosevelt: A Rendezvous with Destiny.* Boston: Little Brown and Company, 1990.

Garraty, John A. *The New Commonwealth 1877-1890.* New York: Harper & Row Inc., 1968.

Gillon, Steven M., and Cathy D. Matson. *The American Experiment: A History of the United States.* Boston: Houghton Mifflin Company, 2002.

Grove, B. Stephen. "The Decline of the Republican Machine in Philadelphia 1936-52, " PhD diss., University of Pennsylvania, 1976.

Guffey, Joseph. *Seventy Years on the Red Fire Wagon*. Privately Printed, 1952.

Hatfield, Eugene. "The Impact of the New Deal on Black Politics in Pennsylvania, 1928-1936." PhD diss., University of North Carolina at Chapel Hill, 1979.

Healy, Robert L. "Interparty Competition in Pennsylvania, 1954-1968: A Historical and Political Perspective." *Pennsylvania History* 37 (October 1970): 352-380.

Hutton Hawks, Ann. *The Pennsylvanian: Joseph R. Grundy*. Philadelphia: Dorrance & Company, 1962.

Keller, Richard C. *Pennsylvania's Little New Deal*. New York: Garland Publishing Inc., 1982.

Kehl, James. "Philadelphia, 1948: City Of Crucial Conventions." *Pennsylvania History* 67 (Spring 2000): 313-326.

Kennedy, John J. *Pennsylvania Elections: Statewide Contests from 1950-2004*. Lanham: University Press of America Inc., 2006.

Klein, Philip S., and Ari Hoogenboom. *A History of Pennsylvania*. University Park: The Pennsylvania State University Press, 1980.

Madonna, G. Terry, and Berwood Yost. *Pennsylvania Votes: Presidential Primaries, 1972-1992: A Sourcebook*. Millersville, Pa.: Millersville University, 1996.

Maiale, Hugo. "The Italian Vote in Philadelphia between 1928 and 1946." PhD diss., University of Pennsylvania, 1950.

Martin, Edward. *Always Be On Time*. Harrisburg: The Telegraph Press, 1958.

McGeary, Nelson H. *Gifford Pinchot: Forester Politician*. Princeton: Princeton University Press, 1960.

McKenna, William. "The Negro Vote in Philadelphia Elections." *Pennsylvania History* 27 (October 1965): 406-415.

McLarnon, John M. *Ruling Suburbia: John J. McClure and the Republican Machine in Delaware County Pennsylvania*. Dover: University of Delaware Press, 2003.

Michener, James. *Report of the County Chairman*. New York: Random House, 1961.

Milkis, Sidney M., and Michael Nelson. *The American Presidency: Origins and Development, 1776-1998*. Washington: Congressional Quarterly Inc., 1999.

Miller, Guy V. "Pennsylvania's Scrambled Politics." *Nation*, May 14, 1938, 555-58.

Murray, Robert K. *The Harding Era*. Minneapolis: University of Minnesota Press, 1969.

Morris, Joe A. "That Guy Duff," *Saturday Evening Post*, August 18, 1951, 115-118.

Murray, Robert K. *The 103rd Ballot: Democrats and the Disaster in Madison Square Garden*. New York: Harper & Row Inc., 1976.

Nelson, Michael, ed. *The Elections of 2004*. Washington: Congressional Quarterly Inc., 2005.

Novak, Robert, D. *The Agony of the G.O.P. 1964*. New York: The Macmillan Company, 1964.

Pepper, George Wharton. *Philadelphia Lawyer: An Autobiography*. Philadelphia: J.B. Lippincott Co., 1944.

Pittenger, John C. *Politics Ain't Beanbag*. Bloomington: Authorhouse, 2005.

Polakoff, Keith I. *Political Parties in American History*. New York: John Wiley & Sons Inc., 1981.

Pomper, Marlene Michaels, ed. *The Election of 1980 Reports and Interpretations*. Chatham: Chatham House Pub. Inc., 1981.

Quay, Matthew Stanley. *Pennsylvania Politics*. Philadelphia: W.J. Campbell, 1901.

Reichley, James A. *States in Crisis*. Chapel Hill, N.C.: University of North Carolina Press, 1964.

Scott, Hugh. *Come to the Party*. Englewood Cliffs, N.J.: Prentice-Hall Inc., 1968.

Sherman, Richard B. *The Republican Party and Black America from McKinley to Hoover, 1896-1933*. Charlottesville: University Press of Virginia, 1973.

Sorauf, Frank. *Party and Representation, Legislative Politics in Pennsylvania*. New York: Atherton Press, 1963.

Specter, Arlen, with Charles Robbins. *Passion for Truth: From Finding JFK's Single Bullet to Questioning Anita Hill to Impeaching Clinton*. New York: Harper Collins Inc., 2000.

Stave, Bruce M. *The New Deal and the Last Hurrah, Pittsburgh Machine Politics*. Pittsburgh: University of Pittsburgh Press, 1970.

Sundquist, James L. *Dynamics of the Party System: Alignment and Realignment of Political Parties in the United States*. Washington: The Brookings Institution, 1983.

Thornburgh, Dick. *Where the Evidence Leads: An Autobiography*. Pittsburgh: University of Pittsburgh Press, 2003.

Treadway, Jack. *Elections in Pennsylvania: A Century of Partisan Conflict in the Keystone State*. University Park: The Pennsylvania State University Press, 2005.

"Two Men Can Determine the G.O.P. Nomination." *New Republic*, June 30, 1952, 6, 17.

Weber, Michael. *Don't Call Me Boss: David L. Lawrence, Pittsburgh's Renaissance Mayor*. Pittsburgh: University of Pittsburgh Press, 1988.

Witcover, Jules. *Party of the People: A History of the Democrats*. New York: Random House, 2003.

White, Theodore H. *The Making of the President 1960*. New York: Atheneum Publishers, 1960.

"Senator Duff of the Eisenhower Team." *New York Times Magazine*, November 11, 1951, 70-71.

Wolf, George D. *William Warren Scranton—Pennsylvania Statesman*. University Park: The Pennsylvania State University Press, 1981.

This Publication is Supported

by a grant from

The Pennsylvania Historical and Museum Commission

Other titles in
the Pennsylvania History Studies Series

To learn more about these titles and to place orders, visit the web site
http://www.pa-history.org/pastudyseries.htm or contact
The Pennsylvania Historical Association
216 Pinecrest, Mansfield University
Mansfield, PA 16933

Featured Titles

Sports in Pennsylvania, by Karen Guenther
Women of Industry and Reform, by Marion Roydhouse
Native Americans' Pennsylvania, by Daniel Richter
Philadelphia: A Brief History, by Roger Simon

The Arts

Pennsylvania's Decorative Arts, by Irwin Richman
Pennsylvania's Painters, by Irwin Richman
Pennsylvania's Architecture (revised edition), by Irwin Richman

Ethnic Series

The Black Presence in Pennsylvania (revised edition), by Emma Lapsansky
The Irish in Pennsylvania, by Dennis Clark
Jewish Life in Pennsylvania, by Dianne Ashton
The Pennsylvania Germans (revised edition), by Charles H. Glatfelter
Polish Presence in Pennsylvania, by Matthew Magda
Scotch-Irish Presence in Pennsylvania, by James H. Smylie

Great Debates

Pennsylvania and the Federal Constitution, edited by Robert G. Crist
Pennsylvania and the Bill of Rights, edited by Robert G. Crist

Industry

The Iron Industry in Pennsylvania, by Gerald G. Eggert

Movers & Shakers

Pennsylvania Kingmakers, edited by Robert G. Crist
Pennsylvania Reformers, by Ira V. Brown